F'D

SPECTACULAR
DOT-COM
FLAMEOUTS

COM-
PANIES

PHILIP J. KAPLAN

SIMON & SCHUSTER

NEW YORK   LONDON   TORONTO   SYDNEY   SINGAPORE

SIMON & SCHUSTER
Rockefeller Center
1230 Avenue of the Americas
New York, NY 10020

For information about special discounts for bulk purchases,
please contact Simon & Schuster Special Sales:
1-800-456-6798 or business@simonandschuster.com

Designed by Bonni Leon-Berman

Manufactured in the United States of America

10   9   8   7   6   5   4   3   2   1

Library of Congress Cataloging-in-Publication Data is available.

ISBN 0-7432-2862-6

FOR MY IMMEDIATE FAMILY—
Mom, Dad, Seth, and Joseph

FOR MY EXTENDED FAMILY—
the thousands of employees who were screwed,
ripped off, tricked, lied to, or otherwise abused by the
companies herein

CONTENTS

CONTENTS

F'D COMPANIES

INTRODUCTION

So a bunch of Internet companies went bust . . . You may think I'm pretty arrogant for claiming to know what their problems were without knowing the first thing about them. And you're probably right. Honestly, I made all this shit up . . . Okay book over stop reading now.

The End

Still, hindsight is 20-20, right?

I mean, who could have guessed that people wouldn't pay big money to read amateur investment advice from complete strangers? (See *iExchange.com*)

Who could have known that we wouldn't rush to trade in our U.S. currency for FLOOZ?

Who knew that consumers wouldn't put a $500 device called "evil" in their kitchens? (See *E Villa*)

And incubators? (See *CampSix*)

Why'd They Fail?

Ask an ex-employee and he'll probably blame management.

Ask management and they'll likely blame the economy.

The economy? MORE VENTURE CAPITAL WAS GIVEN OUT DURING THE FEW YEARS IN WHICH THESE COMPANIES WERE FOUNDED THAN IN THE ENTIRE HISTORY OF AMERICA. BUSINESSES AND CONSUMERS WERE SPENDING RECORD AMOUNTS AND INTERNET USAGE SURPASSED ALMOST ALL PREDICTIONS.

Sure the economy got all fucked up (I'm a financial whiz as you can tell . . .). But it wasn't due to something that *happened*—rather, it was due to a lot of things that *didn't* happen. We *didn't* turn off our radios. We *didn't* abandon our TVs. We *still* go outside to shop most of the time (except me—i don't wear pants).

We laughed at Flooz.

We thought the sock puppet was annoying.

So Then, Why'd They Fail (Part II)?

If run properly, many of these companies could have made it as small, successful businesses. Thing is, "small" wasn't in their vocabulary. You'll find specifics in the rest of this book.

But in general . . . . . .

Too early, too late, too expensive, too cheap, too big, too much competition, too much supply, not enough demand . . . and okay maybe a bit because of management . . . twenty-something Banana-Republic-khaki-pant-wearing Gap-blue-shirt-sporting Stanford-MBA-having Boxster-driving day-trading choad-smoking secretary-ass-palming CEOs.

But we won't discuss them. Nope. I really just wrote that cuz I wanted to use the word "ass-palming."

What Is Ass-Palming?

Far as I can tell, it's like "palming" a basketball—gripping it firmly with one hand. But with ass.

Who Is This Dipshit?

I'm not an analyst, I'm not an investor, I'm not an executive. I'm a computer programmer. I'm that dude at your office in the dark cubicle who nobody listens or pays attention to (especially the hotties in marketing).

On the Internet (yeah I'm cool like that), I go by "Pud." I was thinking about making *Pud* the official author of this book but then I remembered my main motivation for writing it—hanging out in the bookstore picking up chicks.

"Hey waddaya know, they have MY BOOK here. Yes, I wrote it. Uh huh it's true. Now come home with me you MINX."

"You're 'Pud'?"

So now I'm "Philip J. Kaplan." I put the middle initial in there not only cuz I'm a huge *Family Ties* fan, but also because there's apparently some dude who writes World War II novels named Philip Kaplan.

. . . although come to think of it, he prolly scores tons of ass with that stuff . . . oh well too late to change now (as I write this, this book is already for sale on Amazon—it even says how many pages it's gonna be. Miss Cleo must work there.)

Wha? oh yeah.

Fuckedcompany.com

In May of 2000 I built a website called Fuckedcompany .com. That was just around the time when tech markets started to go south. One month earlier, April 2000, is the month generally associated with being the start of the dot-com shit-storm.

Fuckedcompany.com was my attempt at a "bad news only" site about dot-com companies . . . but to keep it stupid (I like stupid. So do you, as evidenced by the book you're now holding in your sticky little fingers), I made it like a "celebrity dead-pool." But instead of betting on celebrity deaths, users bet on the demise of selected companies.

Anyway . . . the site started out pretty much as a joke. I used to read a lot of the tech–news sites, scouring for *bad* dot-com news. Not cuz I'm morbid or anything, but because I'd been waiting for it. I'd been waiting for *something*.

Allow me to explain.

To many people, including myself, the whole dot-com thing was like a murder mystery. You *think* you know who dunnit, but either way, the suspense builds up until you reach the finale. The suspense of watching millions upon millions of dollars being POURED into these startup businesses was gripping—they didn't make any money, so what would happen as the cash started to run out?

Well I'd write a book about it, that's what would happen of course.

And so here I am JACKASS.

When did I get so cynical? A question I've been asked a few times . . . what follows is the short version. If you don't give a fuck (if I were you I probably wouldn't), feel free to skip this section.

So.

Bearded Clam: The BBS Days

In 1989 I was a freshman in high school. Interested in building games and graphics, I'd taught myself a fair amount of computer programming. To fuel my "research," I pulled an extension from my dad's fax line into my bedroom and launched The Bearded Clam (TBC)—a bulletin board system (BBS) on a state-of-the-art Hyundai 386sx computer with 2400 baud modem.

Yeah, Hyundai made PCs at that point. They pretty much sucked as bad as the cars—but were just as cheap.

So if you don't really know what a BBS is, think of it as a website—but instead of dialing into your Internet service provider (ISP) and *then* connecting to the website through your browser, you instead dial *directly* into the website.

Each BBS had a different phone number, and very few BBSs were networked to anything. Kids generally frequented BBSs in their local area code, as to avoid long-distance charges. For that reason, there was demand for similar BBSs in different area codes (wake up—that was foreshadowing . . .). In other words, a BBS in California wasn't competition for a website in New York, even if they were identical.

Like a website, most BBSs allowed users to send email (to other users on that BBS), participate in message boards, chat, play text-based games, and trade files.

Also like websites, most BBSs had a specialty. Gaming, community, porn . . . My BBS specialized in pirated software—specifically, games. As the system operator (SysOp—pretty much equivalent to webmaster), I provided none of the files, but simply kept the server running as users traded files and information.

Fast-forward four years. As a freshman at Syracuse University in 1993, a friend of mine was telling me about this new thing called Mosaic. Developed by Netscape's Marc Andreesen (who later bombed out with LoudCloud; see *Xuma.com*), Mosaic was the first graphical web browser to achieve any sort of popularity.

The First Thing I Said . . .

. . . when I saw a web browser for the first time, no lie, was "Wow! It's like a BBS—but instead of needing, say, a gaming BBS in each *area code*, you only need ONE gaming BBS for the *whole thing!!*"

Because I could access websites all over the world by just dialing a local ISP's phone number, the logical conclusion was *"BBSs will disappear, to be replaced by a very small number of popular websites."*

Look I'm not claiming to be a hotshot or whatever. Just the contrary—I'm an idiot dork. Anyone in my position would have come up with the exact same conclusion. The long-distance barrier was the main obstacle in BBS-land, and now it was GONE! Major consolidation needed.

So you know what happened next . . . ? Ten online pet supply sites, scores of online bookstores, so many sites doing the same fucking thing. The audience was huge but fickle—one mouse click and a new site would load.

New York City

Fast-forward five more years. After an eleven-month stint in Virginia as a twenty-one-year-old consultant with stodgy consultancy Booz Allen & Hamilton, I decided one weekend, on a whim, to move to New York City and find work as a programmer.

Well actually that's a lie—I moved to NYC cuz I wanted to be (and still intend to be) A FAMOUS HEAVY-METAL ROCK-STAR DRUMMER. Yeah I know there haven't been any of those since the mid-eighties, but we're about due.

"Uhh, Grandma [who lives in NYC's Upper West Side], mind if I stay with you for, I dunno, MONTHS [rent is fucking expensive here]?"

So yeah, I moved from Maryland to NYC when I was twenty-two. I scored a job working for Think New Ideas, a "hip" web shop founded in part by ex-MTV VJ Adam Curry, a childhood hero of mine. Adam not only hosted Headbanger's Ball, but he was also the defendant in the first big domain-name dispute, as the original owner of MTV.com.

I took the job at Think because the title had the word "manager" in it—specifically, I was the scrub known as "technical project manager." All of my other offers had been for programming positions, but this one just sounded cooler.

The "Real World"

At Think we did great work. Clients loved us, we loved each other, things were good. The only weird part was that WE WERE CHARGING SO MUCH FUCKING MONEY.

I remember writing a cost estimate for $2,000 and having my manager tell me that the price was too low and to stick another zero on it. Walla—like that I just brought in $18,000 more dollars. Then $40,000. Then $100,000. We once charged about $1 million to a client for about four months' worth of work for four guys.

I think I was making around $55,000 a year at the time—the other guys on the project were probably making about the same. So how four of us charged $1 million for four months' work, I've no idea—but we did.

I remember feeling both guilty and confused. *Guilty* because I *knew* the shit we were doing was easier than the marketing folks would allow the client to know. *Confused* cuz I had no fucking clue where all this money was coming from, or where it was gonna go.

The "Real" Real World

If what I was doing at Think New Ideas was so goddam valuable, what the hell was I doing making only $55,000 a year for?—which of course is nothing to complain about—unless you live in Manhattan, in which case you're eating ramen noodles and drinking Tab. But it wasn't about the money (honest!)—rather, I felt taken advantage of. What the hell.

Which leads me to one of my favorite little screw-fests. When I was first hired by Think New Ideas, I wanted stock options. Why? No clue, but everyone seemed to be getting rich off the buggers. And hell, all the Internet companies were offering them, so why not ask. So anyway, the response from management was "*You will receive stock options after one year of employment with this company.*"

That's clear enough, right? So I waited patiently and worked hard. As my eleventh month of employment rolled around, I went up to the manager who had originally promised my stock options. I explained to him that it had almost been a year since I'd started work there, and that I'd like to "get the ball rolling" on those options.

"What stock options?" the manager asked me.

"Uhh, the options that YOU said I would receive after working here for one year," I replied.

"Oh, right, *those* options."

"So . . . where are they? How do we do this?"

"Well you're not getting them yet," that fuckroast had the nerve to say.

"But you promised."

"No I didn't."

"Yes you did."

"I said you'd get options '*AFTER one year.*' That could mean one year, two years . . . ten years . . ."

And so I turned in my resignation and started freelance programming. My goal was to start a small business by bootstrapping it and eventually hiring four-or-so people to build those "$1 million" websites for, say, 200 grand. We'd make more money, the client would save money, everyone would be happy. And we were, as PK Interactive became a reality, a successful little "Internet boutique."

Fast-forward about one year.

Fuckedcompany.com (Part II)

May 26, 2000. Memorial Day weekend. My consultancy, PK Interactive, was rockin' and rollin'. I had five employees and we were working on projects for Mead Paper, Toyota, and some other companies, large and small. Most of our clients weren't dot-com "pure-plays," but rather were companies using the Internet to expand their existing, offline businesses.

So Memorial Day weekend is a big travel weekend for New Yorkers—but I of course had no plans. Pretty much everyone I knew was out of town and I was bored, home alone, with nothing to do for four days.

Wouldn't that be the perfect time to make that newsy dead-pool site about dot-com companies? Why not.

When it came time to choose a name, the first thing that popped into my head was the magazine *Fast Company*. *Fast Company* was pretty much the opposite of a dot-com deadpool—it worshiped that whole "new economy" thing—my site was their blasphemy.

Fast Company? Fuckedcompany.com, there it was. Being a programmer—not a graphic designer—the first version of the website was *really* ugly (okay fine . . . it's *still* ugly). The original logo was a parody of *Fast Company*'s logo (which the magazine later asked me to change, and being as I didn't much care for the logo in the first place, I complied). The site's background was dark red, to be all evil and bloodlike. As for content, I just copied shit from other news sites on the Internet (shhhh, don't tell anyone).

Three days later, the site was done. Thing was, the day after I finished, I had a trip planned to go to Brazil for a week with some friends. So I showed one of my employees how to update the site while I was gone.

I emailed my new site's address to six friends and took off for Rio, in search of the Girl from Ipanema.

Three days into my trip, I got a message that a reporter from online magazine Salon.com was trying to contact me for an interview about the site.

Wha?

I got back from Brazil to find that over 20,000 people had signed up to play the dead-pool game. I had thousands of emails from dot-com employees informing me of the goings on in their companies. I received email from laid-off dot-commers on the brink of depression, thanking me for the site, explaining that it was therapeutic—one read and they knew they weren't alone and they weren't to blame.

And just a few "cease and desist" letters.

As of this writing, over a year later, about 4 million people visit Fuckedcompany.com each month. *Rolling Stone* picked it as "Hot Site," Yahoo! Internet Life deemed it "Site of the Year," and *Time* magazine even picked it as #6 in their "Best of 2000" issue (damn that Napster kid).

Thousands of premium subscriptions, as well as T-shirts, mouse pads, mugs, and other crap, have been sold through the site. "Per head, it's probably the most profitable company in the history of Silicon Alley," wrote Joseph Gallivan, some crazy Brit, for the *New York Post*. Pip pip! Let's snog.

Terms and Conditions

- What follows is a collection of fucked Internet companies, most of which are out of business. You might notice that some of these sites still seem to exist. Sometimes that's because they're still conducting business, but for the most part, new companies have purchased the domain names of the deceased and have sprouted up in their place—much like how a new store might move into a bankrupt store's previous location and keep the old name. Additionally, the assets of many of these companies have been sold (for pennies on the dollar) and have been reopened under new, hopefully brighter, management.

- The opinions herein incorporate my own, as well as ideas and discussions with former employees and executives in both real life as well as from various online message boards (including but not exclusively Fuckedcompany's Happy Fun Slander Corner).

- Philip J. Kaplan (a.k.a. Pud) is an idiot.

If you agree,
CLICK HERE TO CONTINUE

CHAPTER ONE

TOUGH
SHIP

PETS.COM

I'm out of dog food and my cat's box needs new litter. I know what I'll do: I'll order Dog Chow and Fresh Step on-line from a sock puppet and then I'll watch the dog starve and the cat shit all over the house while I wait for it to be delivered!

Waiting was just part of the problem. Pets.com assumed, probably correctly, that many potential customers would be turned away by high shipping costs. So . . . they only charged $5 shipping for a standard 40-lb. bag of pet food, when actual shipping costs were at least twice that. Similarly, small items like a $2.50 dog bone weren't worth shipping.

Amazon.com, one of Pets.com's major backers, thought they could use their muscle to make Pets.com succeed. Instead, they managed to blow through over $100 million with the help of brilliant purchases such as a $2 million Super Bowl ad and a float in the Macy's Thanksgiving Day Parade. Other investors included the infamous venture capital firms Idealab and Hummer Winblad—the same butt-plugs who brought us Rivals.com, Gazoontite.com, and TheKnot.com.

They should have sold actual pets and shipped them UPS—better margins . . .

Pet Cemetery

At the beginning, there were four: Pets.com, Petstore.com, Petopia.com, and Petsmart.com.

Hilarity ensued.

July 1999	Petopia.com raises $66 million funding
Sept. 1999	Petsmart.com raises $66 million funding
Nov. 1999	Pets.com raises $35 million funding
	Petstore.com raises $97 million funding
Feb. 2000	Pets.com raises $82.5 million more in IPO
June 2000	Pets.com buys Petstore.com
Nov. 2000	Petsmart.com raises $30 million more funding
	Pets.com goes out of business
Dec. 2000	Petco buys Petopia.com's assets
	Petsmart.com buys domain name from Pets.com

WEBVAN

Look, I'm the laziest fucker on Earth. I buy tons of shit on-line, but I still go to the supermarket to buy my food. Although there have been times when I've fantasized about ordering from Webvan just to watch some poor sap unload my groceries while I sit there, watching TV and drinking a beer . . .

Uhh . . . okay so raising and burning through more than $1 BILLION (that's billion with a "B"), the online grocer Webvan gained notoriety as being one of the biggest dot-com failures of 'em all.

The grocery business is a penny operation. Margins are razor thin. The most successful grocery retailers are big chains that buy in bulk, sometimes directly from the manufacturer. Webvan just didn't have the buying power, infrastructure, or demand to compete.

Simply put, Webvan was a classic example of PAYING more for products than they were SELLING them for. There's really not much more to it.

One of the more interesting chapters in the Webvan story has to do with their president, George Shaheen. Shaheen was CEO of Andersen Consulting until the end of October 1999. At the time, companies like Andersen Consulting (now known as Accenture, pronounced "Ass-ENTER") had serious problems with employees leaving in droves to go work for COOL HIP Internet-dot-com-cyber-virtual-e-companies.

So . . . after trying to convince Andersen employees that it was a bad idea to leave and that dot-coms are stupid,

THEIR OWN FUCKIN CEO QUITS to join Webvan.
About eighteen months later, after realizing Webvan's bleak
future (you didn't need a crystal ball . . .), he quit.

KOZMO.COM

Kozmo.com, king of the single-movie-rental-messengered-
to-your-door-with-no-tipping, decided a little too late to require a minimum order.

   If Kozmo were really such a good idea in the first place,
Domino's would have been a $500 billion company ten

years ago . . . Pizza delivery places make money cuz they make a pizza for $1 and sell it for $12. Hand-delivering pints of Ben & Jerry's just ain't the same.

Eventually Kozmo did instate a $10 minimum charge, but then they couldn't find enough customers who wanted 10 bucks' worth of Snickers and *Fight Club* . . . New York rival UrbanFetch.com died for pretty much the same reason—and incidentally didn't have as good a porn selection.

Funny thing is that pretty much EVERY FUCKING STORE in New York City manages to accomplish home delivery without burning through $250 million.

Kozmo's investors included Amazon.com, venture capital firm Flatiron Partners, and evil Starbucks.

Digital Divide

In an unrelated shipping problem, Kozmo was sued in Washington, D.C., because they wouldn't deliver to certain low-income, primarily minority neighborhoods.

Kozmo's excuse was that they're an Internet company, and people living in those neighborhoods don't have computers.

FURNITURE.COM

After spending $2.5 million on their domain name, Furniture .com discovered that UPS wouldn't ship bulky items like sofas and tables, and they were forced to use more expensive shipping alternatives.

"There were many cases when we would get an order for a $200 end table and then spend $300 to ship it. We never could figure it out," one former Furniture.com engineer told CNET's News.com.

Another problem that hit Furniture.com was that some of the small furniture manufacturers they used couldn't keep up with the volume of orders, causing long shipping delays.

The Better Business Bureau in Worcester, Massachusetts, received over forty complaints about the furniture retailer in just two months. "This is an extraordinary number of complaints," said Barbara Sinnott, president of the local BBB, to *The Boston Globe*. "It makes me alarmed."

In total, $75 million was invested into this company. $27 million of it was last-minute venture capital reportedly swindled from investors by taking them on a tour of the facilities while having accountants and engineers pose as busy customer-service representatives, talking to imaginary customers on dead phone lines.

According to Furniture.com's IPO filing—a public offering that never happened—they lost $46.5 million in 1999 alone.

CHAPTER TWO

SOLUTIONS IN SEARCH OF A PROBLEM

EREGISTER.COM

What did eRegister.com do? Well, according to them. . . . . .

"Innovative Registration Solutions."

Translation: You fill out a form, we send an email to the YMCA and Weight Watchers.

"eRegister is leading the way in creating online solutions that focus on the registration needs of active families and individuals. Our website features recognized organizations in your community along with detailed information about the thousands of activities, programs, classes and events they provide."

Yes, about five different organizations. How impressive.

"Register online safely for classes and activities."

As opposed to what? Not safely?

"Link directly to organizers' web sites and so much more!"

FUCK YOU okay?

"eRegister is the flexible and convenient way to access all your activity needs online 24 hours a day 7 days a week."

Yeah, curse those nine-to-five websites!

So anyway . . . eRegister.com reportedly spent more than $5 million keeping what few customers they had happy with this free and stupid service.

The company closed shop in July 2001, due to failed negotiations with the YMCA—and probably the realization that the Internet was a better place without them.

IHARVEST.COM

I don't think I've ever seen a more useless company than iHarvest.com. Actually, I'm sure of it. Such a waste. Shame . . . shame.

Awarded "Editors' Choice" by the goofs at *PC Magazine,* iHarvest was a "storage and retrieval" service. It was a browser plug-in that allowed users to click a button and magically store copies of web pages on iHarvest's server.

I'm serious, that's what it did. No, really. $6.9 million was invested into this company by people who apparently weren't aware that Internet Explorer and Netscape ALREADY DO THIS. THERE'S A FUCKIN "SAVE" OPTION UP ON THE TOP OF YOUR BROWSER, promise.

But WAIT, there's MORE! If you just wanted to store the URL, and not the actual text and graphics, you could do that too! Amazing! I mean . . . why bother using your browser's built-in FAVORITES or BOOKMARKS function when you can register on iHarvest.com and install their software? It's FUN to install software!

I must admit that iHarvest's new-economy-bullshit-speak was some of the best I've seen. Whoever wrote this has a gift. *"[iHarvest.com] provides integrated technology that radically improves the productivity of information-centric businesses by expanding their information solutions to incorporate Web-based and other underutilized digital resources."*

They discontinued service on September 28, 2001.

THIRD VOICE

I've heard a lot of ridiculous dot-com ideas and business plans, but this one was so inane that when I first heard of it, it actually pissed me off.

Third Voice was a free little browser plug-in you could download that would enable you to put virtual "sticky notes" on websites (see *Sticky Networks*). As a Third Voice user, you could see all the sticky notes that everyone before you had posted. It was supposed to make the Web more "interactive."

Being the hooligan that I am, it seemed to me right away that the only practical application for such technology was to vandalize other websites—virtual graffiti. Apparently I wasn't the only one who thought so—Third Voice sticky notes quickly degenerated into almost exclusively bitchy, cynical comments.

Much like this book.

Anyway, almost immediately upon the launch of Third Voice's service, controversy broke out. A lot of webmasters didn't like the technology, as they imagined a world where *everyone* used Third Voice sticky notes, and webmasters would lose control of their sites.

Didn't matter, it sucked—especially if you were one of the investors who pumped $15 million into this toy. Most people who installed the software tried it for a few minutes before the novelty wore off.

The CEO—who happened to be one of the inventors of the chewy granola bar when she was with Quaker Oats (those, too, make me sick)—shut down the service on April 2, 2001.

WWWRRR.COM

Okay, the first issue we have to discuss here is the issue of their name. Wwwrrr.com. Pronounced "whir." Stands for "World Wide Web reading, 'riting, 'rithmetic." That's just wrong. On so many levels.

Anyway, all that doesn't matter anymore cuz they're fucked. That's right. Let's explore.

According to their eyesore of a site, Wwwrrr.com was *"a fun, friendly place for parents, teachers, and kids to learn, explore, shop and connect."* Specifically, they worked with schools to create sites for parents and teachers with information ranging from class schedules and homework to sports scores and club meetings.

Yeah, loads of money to be made there. The company scored $15 million funding from some apparently generous yet gravely misguided investors—it wasn't a business, it was fucking charity. And why pay Wwwrrr to build you a website when you can probably get little Johnny's fourteen-year-old brother to do it for you?

And I dunno, when I was a kid, we had a piece of paper taped to the refrigerator that seemed to work just fine. Was there some piece of information I was missing that validated the existence of a $15 million company? Probably not.

Wwwrrr employed about 120 people. They ceased operations on January 10, 2001, when they couldn't find the reported $30 million MORE that they needed to stay in business and IPO.

lol.

HR

As was all too common during the dot-com meltdown, Wwwrrr.com's laid-off employees were screwed big time. Besides wiping their asses with their stock options, ex-employees alleged they weren't paid for their last two weeks and never received their final expense reimbursements.

Yet another suit brought on by employees, yet another Labor Department investigation.

EMARKER

Now here's something the world was screaming for.

From their site: "*eMarker.com solves the most frustrating part of hearing a song on the radio—not knowing the title of the song or the name of the artist who's just captured your attention. eMarker enables music lovers to connect the music they hear on their local radio stations with information and resources on the Internet.*"

Okay that's fancy for A 20-DOLLAR DEVICE THAT BASICALLY DID NOTHING BUT RECORD THE TIME YOU PUSHED A BUTTON.

eMarker, a wholly owned subsidiary of Sony (see *E Villa*), was just that—a little keychain thing with a button on it. Hear a song you like on the radio and push the button.

Go home, plug the thing into your computer, log in to eMarker.com, tell it what radio station you were listening to, and it would tell you the name of the song you were listening to. That is, if the radio station was monitored by Broadcast Data Systems (BDS).

Sorta off-topic here, but you should know just how cool BDS is. It's a company that sets up computers all over the country for monitoring radio stations. Each of these computers is connected to a database that contains audio samples of thousands of different songs. The BDS computers "listen" to the radio all day and log the different songs that the stations are playing.

And then they sell this information to assnecks like eMarker.

Apparently Sony didn't expect to make a ton of dough from selling the actual device—rather, the "money" was in both advertising, as well as commissions from people buying the music they found on eMarker.com . . . but I think Napster (well . . . Gnutella . . .) solved *that* problem . . .

Anyway, I have two new ideas that can fill the void left by the departure of eMarker:

1) A "phone"—This high-tech device enables you to call the radio station you were just listening to and ask them what song it is they were just playing.

2) "Friends"—No, not the TV show, but this new networking principle will enable you to ask one of your "friends" if they've heard a certain song. Simply recite the lyrics you heard or hum the melody to retrieve a possible match.

Sony shut the service down on September 30, 2001. Possibly to avoid negative karma points, Sony announced they would buy back used eMarkers for $25. Props.

COLO.COM

Colo.com was supposed to build a new type of colocation service. Colocation is web hosting, where instead of using servers owned by the hosting company, the servers are owned by you and are only located at the hosting company's datacenter, using their Internet connection and sometimes their support staff.

Colo.com built datacenters all around the country, mostly in secondary markets. The thing is, EVERYBODY was building datacenters. When dot-coms went into the toilet, guess what . . . millions of unused square feet.

Worse yet, Colo.com sold datacenter space, cooling, and power, but not bandwidth. In other words, if you wanted to actually hook your server up to the Internet, you would have to talk to them about getting a third-party ISP to help you out. This seriously complicated matters when all people really wanted was a friggin hot network cable to plug into the back of their server. Another issue is that apparently some of their datacenters didn't provide 24/7x365 access to the datacenter, which is problematic if you run, say, a WEBSITE.

Starting with $500 million in venture capital, Colo.com filed Chapter 11 bankruptcy in May 2001, with about $360 million in debt. Their datacenters were sold at auction for pennies on the dollar, and their domain name has been sold to a party that's currently trying to revive the company.

IMPRESSE

The idea behind Impresse, a joke that managed to burn nearly $90 million, was to act as a middleman between printers and print buyers, taking a 1% commission fee for enabling print buyers to "shop around." In turn, print buyers would theoretically save time and money.

What Impresse didn't understand is that print buyers *already* manage to shop around. Using Impresse, going to their silly little site and filling out their silly little forms, resulted in nothing but extra time and work—not to mention the 1% commission.

In other words . . . there are like 60,000 fucking printing companies in the U.S., all of which compete on price in every market. Along comes a bunch of kids in cubicles going where they're not needed, trying to shove this piece of shit down buyers' throats.

Ain't gonna happen.

Additionally, Impresse spent a fortune of time and money creating "official" alliances with established companies like Oracle, Cisco, and Adobe that delivered nothing but bullshit press releases that are worth bull puckies in the Valley . . .

Finally, it's a mystery as to whether Impresse actually created a product or not. It would be a shame to think that two years and $90 million were spent without a single product being fully deployed, but that's how it seems. I have yet to hear from a satisfied customer, *any* customer really . . . but I *have* heard from plenty of companies who were inundated with Impresse's PowerPoint presentation pitches—but nary an actual working demo.

This looked like an IPO play, plain and simple. IPO, cash out, run. Never worked though, people caught on to their game too quick.

In May 2001, competitor PrintCafe.com bought Impresse's remaining assets.

CALENDARCENTRAL.COM

Why would an application service provider like Calendar-Central.com, a site that provides private, shared online calendars for group scheduling, go out of business?

Microsoft Outlook/Exchange you say? Microsoft's calendaring application is pretty much ubiquitous. Of course, it requires Windows, and is proprietary.

So CalendarCentral could target those *other* people, right? People who for whatever reason can't run Microsoft Outlook . . . ?

Right. That tiny, tiny percentage of offices that don't use Microsoft products.

Another one assimilated by the Borg . . . and Microsoft probably didn't even notice.

POPULARPOWER.COM

Unless you're rendering graphics for the next *Toy Story* movie, your computer is underutilized.

That's the basis for distributed computing—pooling spare processing power from networked computers to collectively work on CPU-intensive programming jobs.

I first became a proponent of distributed computing when I ran "SETI@Home." Organized by the Search for

ExtraTerrestrial Intelligence (SETI), the program was essentially a screen saver that would analyze signals from space, looking for signs of intelligent life, while I was away from my computer.

Funded with $1.6 million and employing fourteen people, PopularPower.com thought they could make money from this. They had an application, for example, that would crunch numbers, looking for a flu vaccine. A noble cause, but one that didn't pay the bills.

Two things they could have tried but didn't:

1) Charge companies to use PopularPower's distributed-computing network. Pay PopularPower users a cut and keep a cut for themselves.

2) Sell the technology to large corporations. A large company could force their employees to participate with their work computers, using their extra processing power for the good of the company.

SETI has yet to find intelligent life. And so on.

CAPACITYWEB.COM

Funded with $4.5 million from incubator Devine Interventures, CapacityWeb.com attempted to create a system for manufacturing companies to lease their downtime in order to remain at full capacity.

The idea is that, if you're a manufacturer and your factory isn't making anything, even for a minute, you're losing potential revenue. Manufacturers work to align supply and demand between their suppliers and customers, striving for the manufacturers nirvana—100% uptime.

Enter two fresh-faced college graduate dot-com gold-rushing founders. Once again, we have founders who knew little of the industry they were attempting to "revolutionize."

Turned out manufacturers were more interested in fine-tuning their relationships with existing suppliers and customers, rather than building new relationships—which was the focus of CapacityWeb.

Hanging their heads in shame, the company folded.

REFER.COM

Another terrible idea from the people at Internet incubator idealab![SM] Here's how this scam was supposed to work: Employers post job openings for a fee, and anyone who successfully refers somebody for the job earns a referral bonus of $1,000 or more.

So . . . in contrast, in order of importance, here's how most companies hire people:

1) Internal referrals—Employees or stakeholders refer their friends and acquaintances. Even if the company you work for were offering a huge referral bonus, you'd still be hesitant to refer Bubba, your friend with corn in his teeth, for the sales manager position because it would ultimately reflect poorly on *you.*

2) External recruiters—Headhunters might be shit-shoveling pond scum, but they sometimes have value. Employers may have good relationships with certain recruiters, trusting their judgment. At the very least, you'd expect a recruiter to *somewhat* prescreen each applicant, as to not tarnish their reputation.

3) Solicited applicants—An employer puts an ad in the paper or on a job site. Motivated job seekers match a few keywords and send along their résumés.

4) Unsolicited applicants—Job seekers send résumés to employers who have not asked for them. These applicants are viewed either as having a genuine interest in the company, or as being desperate. Usually the latter.

213) Refer.com—Somebody whom the employer doesn't trust and has never met, refers somebody that *they* don't trust and have never met. The person whose résumé gets passed along doesn't even know they're applying for the job. Random people scour résumé banks and refer thousands of people, hoping to get a hit. Employers get inundated with the lowest-quality applicants possible.

IAM.COM

You don't have to do any market research to know that the supply of actors in Hollywood is far greater than the demand. Ya know . . . where do you think porn stars come from? Makes you wonder what magical fantasy planet the founders and investors of Iam.com were living on, being as they spent around $48 million trying to build a company that WOULD DO THE EXACT OPPOSITE OF WHAT THE INDUSTRY NEEDED.

Iam.com allowed models and actors to create online portfolios, and then thought they could charge casting directors to browse the database.

Essentially, Iam.com's mission was to cut out the middlemen—talent agencies—and connect models and actors directly with casting people. Problem is, casting directors LIKE talent agencies. The whole point of talent agencies is to filter talent for clients, making their lives easier.

The last thing a casting director needs is 100,000 unfiltered headshots pushed their way from low-rate actors who are known to no one as more than simply an entry in a database.

Financed with almost $50 million and employing over sixty people, the site was about as useful as posting "Looking for somebody to star in the new Speilberg movie!" on a Yahoo! message board. Had Spike Lee, one of Iam.com's board members, tried this approach before getting involved, I'm fairly sure he wouldn't have wasted his time on this dog.

As far as actors, if you can't get in with a real talent agency, time to consider learning Java or something . . .

Scapefish

Iam.com made headlines when they sued their web agency, Razorfish, claiming that the site developed by Razorfish had "grave technical and navigational problems which caused severe injury to Iam.com's business."

Shortly after, Razorfish counter-sued, claiming that
Iam.com approved all of Razorfish's work but essentially
stopped paying when they ran into cash-flow problems.
Razorfish said they were owed just over $573,000—and
they prevailed.

I'm sort of torn here. On one hand, there's no fucking way
in hell that Iam.com's business would have worked, pretty
colors or not. It's clear that they were just trying to use
Razorfish as a scapegoat. Wouldn't you feel like a fuck-
face if you flushed $48 million of other people's money
down the toilet on an idea this stupid?

On the other hand, all those big web shops are somewhat
guilty and partially responsible for getting us into this mess
in the first place. I'm assuming that more than a million
bucks, probably a lot more, traded hands on this one.
Blasphemy. The front-end technology behind 95% of the
million-dollar websites out there could be built by any high
school kid with a basic grasp of programming and design.

Of course there's always gonna be a market for good,
old-fashioned management consultants. But let's face it,
most of these companies just build friggin *websites*.

I'm an idiot and even *I* managed to build Fuckedcompany
in a weekend.

MERCATA.COM

This was yet another dot-com set to ROCK THE WORLD OF RETAIL and put all the old-fashioned guys out of business. The thing is, even the press bought into this one. Maybe it's because it was backed and cofounded by Microsoft cofounder (and Seattle SuperSonics owner and Jimi Hendrix museum proprietor, among other things) Paul Allen.

Mercata was one of many "group buying" sites that were oh so popular. The idea behind online group buying is that consumers would use the site to band together and purchase merchandise at wholesale prices. Specifically, a user would log in, find a product he or she was interested in, and tell Mercata how much they were willing to pay for it. The more people who signed up, the cheaper the product got.

Basically, they were middlemen who couldn't get anyone—buyers or sellers—interested.

The company relied on product manufacturers. A lot of manufacturers were reluctant to participate in online group buying programs because of "channel conflict"—the classic e-commerce obstacle where normal distribution channels, for example retail stores, get pissed when manufacturers sell directly to the consumer.

As for buyers, frankly, it just wasn't worth the effort to save just $5 on a stupid toaster. Mercata was, like, twice as annoying as an online auction, which can be quite annoying, because here users had no way of guaranteeing or controlling whether they'd actually end up winning the product.

Finally, cuz so many online retailers were selling at or below cost, Mercata ultimately couldn't save users all that much money, if anything.

The founders and initial investors must have been kicking themselves for their bad timing—they were all set to go with a $100 million IPO in March 2000, just one month before the public wised up, realized what was going on, and the market tanked.

Mercata quickly announced the cancellation of their IPO and, one day later, went out of business.

$89 million and 100 employees were burned.

BIZBUYER.COM

As one of the many "reverse auction" sites poised to take over the online services industry, BizBuyer.com allowed service providers to bid on contract jobs ranging from house painting to software development. The winning bidder was to do the job and share the spoils with BizBuyer.com.

One of the problems with this is that, for many service providers, BizBuyer.com's fee would have taken most of the profit.

One of BizBuyer.com's backers was the incubator eCompanies—the same geniuses who paid $7.5 million for the domain name "Business.com" only to flush it down the toilet months later.

According to the CEO (from their "we're fucked" press release), "*We built a great team and a great service. Unfortunately, we could not build the liquidity and transaction volume necessary to support an ongoing marketplace, as well as create acceptable returns for our investors in today's financial market environment.*"

IT DOESN'T MATTER HOW GREAT YOUR TEAM WAS! Talent doesn't keep you in business—paying customers do. The only thing wrong with the "financial market environment" is that he wasn't able to flip this turd and run to the islands with his millions.

$68 million and 170 employees later, it died.

FOODOO.COM

There are few things more unneeded in this world than more cookbooks—Amazon.com carries over 8,500 of them. British site FooDoo.com (rhymes with "doodoo" har har) was one more, just a collection of recipes.

It was a *free* site, advertising supported, with the goal of turning traffic into revenue. The idea that I'm gonna read a recipe site every day—what fucking planet did these people think we were living on?

And they spent HOW MUCH money to set up and run a recipe file? Hell, my GRANDMOTHER could get my dad to copy her recipes onto a web page and pay him in pecan pies.

We all know that Brits just boil everything, anyway. £1,000,000 in funding down the tubes (I'll let you do the math).

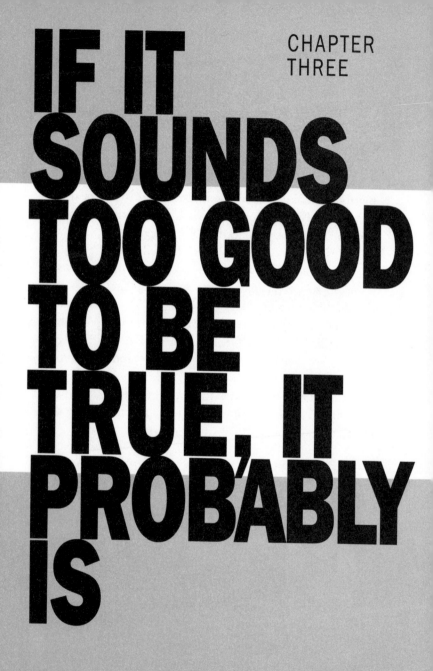

IF IT SOUNDS TOO GOOD TO BE TRUE, IT PROBABLY IS

FANDOM.COM

Don't you love it when big bad companies pretend to be "cool"? Pretend to be "hip"? They're usually exposed, as was Fandom.com.

The Internet was founded by geeks. The first settlers of the Web were geeks. It's no surprise that the first big communities on the Internet revolved around *Star Trek*, *X-Files*, and *The Simpsons*.

"Hey, did you know they have the Internet for computers now?"
—Homer Simpson

As web usage became more widespread, Hollywood studios started cracking down on "fan sites," citing them for stealing logos and other such nonsense.

Enter Fandom.com.

The idea behind Fandom seemed somewhat respectable—bring a slew of fan sites under Fandom's umbrella to provide them with the legal and business services necessary to protect them from studio censorship. Revenue would be generated by selling ads and merchandise.

"By the fans, for the fans," was their slogan.

Which was odd, because they sent legal letters threatening to sue Fandom.TV, a site created by superfan Carol Burrell that was a central portal to her collection of fan sites dating back to 1993.

Fandom.com claimed trademark infringement. Not only were these hypocritical dicks going against everything they "stood for," but they didn't make up the fucking word "fandom," which, according to Webster, dates back to 1903.

FUNBUG.COM

FunBug.com spent over $3 million of investor money creating annoying Java-based online games that let users earn "Fun Bugs" by playing, winning, and beating high scores. Fun Bugs could be transferred and converted to money on "FunCards," which could be spent anywhere MasterCard is accepted.

So yeah, basically they were giving away cash to play their games. And crappy games at that. In the age of PlayStation, Xbox, Unreal, and Lara Croft's boobs, there's no way kids would actually play these games for *fun* . . .

So why'd they play?

You could CHEAT at the games! A burgeoning underground of teenagers figured out cheats, patterns, and solutions to the games and posted them all over the Net—just search Google.com for the keywords "funbug cheat."

So here we have a company with $3 million in funding giving away free money to teenagers with enough time to come cheat on their games. Uh-oh, messy indeed.

Was there even a plan to make money? FunBug marketed themselves as a "direct marketing company that primarily targeted teenagers." You guessed it—advertising.

FunBug's CEO told Internet.com that older folks shouldn't feel left out. "We think people thirty-five and older will love playing. It'll make them feel like they're in their twenties again."

How does playing a fucked-up cheatable Java game of checkers makes middle-aged people feel like they're "in their twenties"?

Their good-bye site blamed "market conditions" for their

demise—and said that people with balances on their Fun-Cards "will be able to access your cash prizes soon . . ."

Don't hold your breath, although as of this writing, it looks as if they're trying to give it another go.

VITESSA.COM

Remember "content is king"? The hilarious notion that whoever delivers the most text, sound, and video would be the RULER OF THE INTERNET? That lasted for a couple of years . . . then sales became "king" and most content sites realized that they had to *sell* stuff to survive. Banner ads, subscriptions, and affiliate links weren't working. Vitessa was one of a large number of companies hoping to cash in from the rude awakening.

Vitessa was a contextual commerce system. They called themselves a "content service provider." Roughly, they provided two services.

1) Vitessa Commerce Platform—Content sites would run their content through Vitessa's system and the user would be presented with relevant shopping links. Users could then shop without leaving the original site (see *ePod.com* for a similar attempt). For example, visit a site related to a particular music artist and a pop-up window selling related books, CDs, and merchandise might appear.

2) Outsource e-Commerce Fulfillment—Supply chain, fulfillment. The works. Vitessa generally bought the products wholesale themselves on what they called "virtual consignment," selling pretty much whatever they thought their clients wanted to sell, to whoever wanted to buy it.

So the idea was basically to turn content sites into e-commerce sites. How many content sites actually made real money off of e-commerce transactions? Apparently fewer than Vitessa expected—they were known for hiring huge numbers of people based on outlandish sales forecasts.

Many companies offered the same, similar, or alternate solutions (ePod, YellowBrix, Pop2It, FizzyLab, Iconomy, Escelate, and even CafePress.com to name a few). Competition was fierce and margins were small—Vitessa had to split earnings between the wholesaler, themselves, and their clients.

Vitessa's clients were relatively small sites, as it made more sense for larger sites to build their own e-commerce infrastructures to avoid Vitessa's 30% to 70% fee. What this meant to Vitessa, besides clients potentially fleeing as their sites grew, was that they didn't sell huge amounts of product, so they couldn't negotiate bulk prices the way a company like Amazon could. In other words . . . consumers didn't want to buy cuz Vitessa's prices were too high.

There was also a major obstacle in getting sites to sign up. Vitessa had to convince client sites to let an outsider sell goods in their name. If Vitessa screwed anything up, the originating site would seem responsible even though the e-commerce sections of their site were largely out of their control. Not to mention that by the time these content sites started trying e-commerce, it was generally a move out of desperation, and many of Vitessa's clients were already on their way out.

Vitessa employed untold hundreds and had offices in Seattle, San Francisco, New York, Chicago, and San Diego. Before they shut down, the slogan on their website read, *"Vitessa has helped some of the world's most recognizable companies build successful online businesses."*

Ya know?

ONLINECHOICE.COM

OnlineChoice.com's purpose (other than to generate content for this book) was to help consumers get good deals on things like electricity, natural gas, long distance, local telephone service, Internet access, and home security. Demand aggregation—round up enough people who all want the same thing and broker a better deal, buying and paying in bulk, saving everyone money.

Sounds familiar? It is . . . it's basically another group buying fiasco (see *Mercata.com*) but this time with fewer products and less savings. And this one cost investors around $20 million and employed seventy people. Seventy people. This business, this WEBSITE, could have been run by a SCRIPT. Zero employees. Okay MAYBE a couple of people to broker the deals with suppliers . . .

Funny thing about OnlineChoice.com is that the offers were plain uninteresting. They had to do the impossible—get customers to sign up and accept offers for 0% to 5% savings. Anyone with half a brain could figure out that they would only be saving a whopping $20 per year on most offers. Not worth the time filling out their stupid little forms . . .

The founder of OnlineChoice.com was picked as "Entrepreneur of the Year" by Ernst & Young. In February 2001, OnlineChoice.com's founder told the press that prospects were so bright he turned down a $300 million offer to buy the company.

Three months later the company declared Chapter 7 bankruptcy with an estimated $10 million in debt. OnlineChoice.com's remains were later purchased by an investor for $70,000.

Rock on.

EFANSHOP.COM

eFanShop.com was the company with the terrible domain name that set up sports merchandise e-commerce stores on sports-related content sites.

For example, let's say you have a site devoted to your favorite basketball players. You contract eFanShop.com to run your e-commerce. You make the real profits, while eFanShop gets a small commission for taking care of the TECHNOLOGY and the LOGISTICS, usually the two most complex, time-consuming, and expensive parts of running a small- to medium-size e-commerce site.

For the content sites, this was an offer way too good to refuse. Make all the $$$ and leave the hard part to a bunch of suckers.

And if it *sounds* too good to be true . . . well . . .

They had it totally backward. By taking the crappiest job

and getting the smallest cut, it's a wonder their $5 million in venture capital lasted as long as it did—less than one year.

ELETTER.COM

The U.S. Postal Service estimates that the yearly cost of postage alone for mass mailings is over $6 billion! There are over 10 million small- and medium-size companies that send out mass mail! Over 90% of these companies manage their mailings themselves, manually, due to a lack of affordable alternatives!

Funded-out-the-ass with over $23 million, eLetter.com promised to print, fold, stuff, address, and MAIL your JUNK mail. They'd even save you more than 50% on printing costs!

Most small businesses are turned away from mailing houses cuz their quantities are too low—but not eLetter.com. They'd mail as little as fifty freakin' postcards if you wanted them to. All you had to do to get started is fill out a silly little form on their website.

Who cares if they were competing with the United States Postal Service, which has a similar service called Net-Post? eLetter even offers an UNCONDITIONAL 30-day MONEY-BACK guarantee!

eLetter.com was a company that tried to automate the delivery of junk mail.

Turns out thousands of businesses opted to hire high-school kids to stuff envelopes. The post office mailed 'em. They had the right idea. Over 100 employees later, eLetter .com went out of business.

EXTREME CHAMPIONSHIP WRESTLING

It's not a dot-com and really has nothing to do with the Internet, but ECW fucking ruled.

That is all.

CHAPTER FOUR

MESSY ENDINGS

SWAPIT.COM

So let me get this straight:

1) I send them a CD.

2) They give me useless "SwapIt Bucks."

3) They go out of business.

4) I get nothing.

Great, sign me up!

SwapIt.com was a fiercely stupid idea. The premise was that people could trade used CDs and video games with one another by physically mailing their crap to SwapIt.com. Users would then be issued "SwapIt Bucks" that they could use to buy other people's crap that had also been sent to the company.

SwapIt had the ol' "don't-make-a-profit-selling-stuff-but-make-money-from-shipping-and-handling" revenue model that was so prevalent among their peers. Get $3 in SwapIt Bucks, and you could buy another used CD for $3.

Okay, eBay's entire success is based on the fact that they have NO INVENTORY. By dealing with all the inventory and fulfillment, SwapIt is like all of the crap with none of the benefit.

Not to mention a warehouse filled with old John Tesh and Yanni CDs.

Getting back to what we were discussing earlier, what happened if you sent them your CD collection and then hadn't redeemed your SwapIt Bucks before they went out of business?

"According to the Terms and Conditions of Use, transfer of title of ownership occurred upon acceptance of the goods by SwapIt."

Furthermore, *"SwapIt Bucks . . . are not redeemable for cash under any circumstances whatsoever. Since SwapIt is now closed, credits are not able to be redeemed and are gone."*

Translation: "Too bad, so sad."

I believe this is the only dot-com that actually had people SENDING them product and they STILL couldn't stay in business.

FREERIDE.COM

FreeRide was supposed to be to the Web as frequent flyer miles are to airlines. FreeRide was in the business of rewarding customers for time and money spent surfing—specifically, clicking on ads and filling out surveys.

"Surfing." Why is the term "surf" used to describe an action that could more accurately be described as "navigating," "wandering," or even better, "looking at shit"? A long time ago some marketing fuckwad decided that surfing is a sport where one could go anywhere one desired. Not so—when one surfs, one is dependent upon the movement of the wave, right?

Anyway . . . so yeah FreeRide . . . one of the more popular "rewards" they promoted was paying your ISP bill. Free ISP, of course, only valid with participating ISPs. But hey, even Earthlink and InfiNet signed up . . . but why wouldn't they—they're getting paid either way (by FreeRide, those dummies . . .).

Of course, free ISP services weren't hard to come by . . .

Other rewards included gift certificates from companies like Kodak, Clairol, and Johnson & Johnson.

FreeRide was actually pretty popular . . . they blamed their own demise on the fact that they weren't receiving money/awards from companies fast enough to send them out to users. But with $42 million in funding, that seems unlikely . . .

When they finally called it quits, FreeRide screwed users by giving them zero warning that their accumulated points would soon be unusable. *"We're sorry we had to act so quickly!"* it was explained on FreeRide's site.

If only I could get points for pulling meat to porn sites . . . you heard me.

THEMESTREAM.COM

ThemeStream.com allowed users to post original articles about any subject. The company generated revenue from ads, and authors were paid a fixed amount by ThemeStream every time a user viewed their article.

Such a simple concept, makes you wonder how they could fuck it up. I mean, they'd have to do something *really* stupid like pay authors MORE than they were bringing in from ads, right?

This fuckblintz did just that.

They were originally paying authors 10 cents per view, which comes out to an insane $100 CPM (cost per thousand, the standard way of calculating per-view payments). Even during the online advertising heyday, this was way more than advertisers were generally willing to pay. ThemeStream apparently thought they could pay authors a dime, take in a nickel from advertisers, and make money on volume.

After eating it for a while, ThemeStream lowered payments to 2 cents per view. Still more than they'd make off advertising, but it was a step in the right direction. Too little, too late—authors became nervous and many stopped contributing to the site.

Maybe I'm an idiot (okay fine I'm definitely an idiot), but why didn't they just pay authors a *percentage of revenue* rather than a fixed price per view? Of course, they'd still have been screwed if either (a) people stopped submitting articles or (b) the advertising market crumbled—both of which happened.

When ThemeStream ceased operations, they screwed authors. *"We believe it is very unlikely that we will be able to pay any other creditors—including contributors,"* read their site.

EXCHANGEPATH.COM

ExchangePath.com was a "person-to-person" payment site similar to PayPal.com.

Users could create accounts on the site and use their credit card to deposit money into it. Users could then send money from their ExchangePath account to any other user's ExchangePath account. To withdraw from an account, users had to fill out an online form and ExchangePath would mail out a check for the requested amount.

Like a bank, the company generated revenue from transaction fees as well as from interest accrued. 'Twas a useful service, and it was used extensively for online person-to-person transactions, the most popular being eBay. Basically, it was a way to email money to somebody—kinda cool.

But . . . ExchangePath and services like it were heavily targeted by credit-card scammers (see *"Money Shot,"* p. 168).

Before these services existed, all one could do with a stolen credit card was buy stuff. Thief wanted cash, thief had to fence the goods. ExchangePath became the perfect credit card–to–cash converter. Set up two accounts—one as the "payer" and one as the "payee," transfer stolen credit-card money to one, withdraw from the other.

Many person-to-person payment sites accepted transactions from outside the U.S., making them perfect for international credit-card cracking rings that were untouchable by the U.S. justice system.

Some credit-card thieves were so hard-core that they acquired CD-ROMs full of stolen credit-card numbers and wrote scripts to automatically set up accounts for each number. If even a small percentage of the numbers worked, they were in the money.

Funded by incubator CMGI, it's widely believed that ExchangePath's demise was due in part to credit-card fraud. To my knowledge, they've never confirmed or denied the rumors.

CASHWARS.COM

CashWars.com was a free online role-playing game that (supposedly, although rarely witnessed) awarded real money to players. Almost as stupid as "get paid to surf," CashWars actually had a large following—the point, of course, was to make players ultimately look at advertisements.

But, as these things go, fans of the game eventually developed applications, bots, that played the game for them while they were away—accumulating points and money. So here were thousands of halfwits running bots to collect "cash" from a mindless "game" with nonexistent graphics, strategy, game-play, or revenue generating potential.

To make things even more funny, players started hawking their accomplished user accounts on eBay—apparently making more money than they were from the game.

May 30, 2001, the game ended.

As of this writing, they say that they're gonna launch again in the near future . . . then again, that's what they all say. . . . . .

LOGICTIER

LogicTier was an "outsourced infrastructure" business. That's sort of a combination of the following:

• A hosting facility: They simply rent out space, bandwidth, and air conditioning. An example of such a company would be the industry-leading, but Chapter 11–bankrupt, Exodus Communications.

• A managed services company: They maintain networks, routers, security, backups, and generally make sure their customers' servers are up and running. An example would be Hostcentric, who does a FINE job of keeping Fuckedcompany's ghetto-ass web servers from melting (mad phat props, yo).

• A web development agency: You know what they do. They make websites. (See *MarchFirst*)

By both doing stuff in-house as well as utilizing various strategic partners, LogicTier could supposedly accomplish all this stuff so their clients didn't have to. Now, I'm all for outsourcing your technical infrastructure—if you sell shoes online, you're in the SHOE business, not the WEB HOST-ING business. You must have high-level technical people on staff, but leave that other shit up to the professionals.

That said, it was inevitable that LogicTier would be fucked. Allow me to dissect the dominoes.

Hosting companies became fucked not only because they overcompensated just before the dot-com bubble burst, but also because they're on the wrong side of Moore's Law.

Moore's Law states that, basically, computing power doubles every eighteen months. What that means is what takes you eight servers to accomplish today, will only take you four servers eighteen months from now, then two, then one, then eBay will be hosted wirelessly on the CEO's wrist-watch . . .

Anyway, as technology progresses, business for hosting facilities (who make their money by renting physical space for servers) decreases. Seeing this trend a mile away (or maybe eighteen months away) hosting companies started to branch out into the managed services business. Some of-fered managed services themselves while some bought or partnered with managed services companies.

Torched

The year was 1999 and planning began for the 2002 Winter Olympics in Salt Lake City. It was the dot-com heyday. Every friggin Internet company wanted a piece of the action. Many offered their services for free, accepting the honor of being an official Olympic sponsor in lieu of payment.

One such company was LogicTier. In August 1999, they were picked to host and maintain the complex server network for the official Olympic website, SaltLake2002.com.

"It's not an accident that this is being announced eighteen months before the games," one of LogicTier's VPs told the press. "It's going to take eighteen months to be precise in the execution of this. We will be very prepared."

Well too fucking bad for the Olympics, cuz roughly seven months from the start of the games, LogicTier basically closed and had to pull out of the deal.

Incidentally, sports site Quokka.com was supposed to provide the site's content. Quokka also pulled out, declaring bankruptcy in April 2001.

As if competition weren't already harsh enough with competitors including dorks like LoudCloud and Totality and monsters like EDS and IBM, now hosting facilities are in the business.

Saturated.

Starting with $90 million in funding from venture capitalists, including the ever-fucked Kleiner Perkins, LogicTier ditched their customers, laid off almost all of their 210 employees, and "changed their business model." What that means no one seems to know. As of this writing, they no longer have a website.

MYSPACE.COM

What's weirder than being in the "business" of giving away free disk space to over 9 million people? The fact that there was competition.

Driveway.com, Xdrive.com, Freeway.com, and FreeDrive .com were just a few of the companies vying for the opportunity to give you FREE DISK SPACE on their file servers. Their brilliant plan to make money was from both the lucrative (ha) banner ad market, as well as going for the ol' switch-a-roo—get you hooked then start charging. (You know, like how they depict drug dealers in those "keep your kids off drugs" commercials. Incidentally, no drug dealer has ever given me free drugs. False advertising.)

Anyway, what they found out was that pretty much everyone used their service for two things: (1) trading warez (pirated software), and (2) hiding porn from their wives.

Word is that out of their 9 million customers, only around 6,000 or so were willing to pay for the service. Why? I dunno . . . a 30GB Maxtor from Best Buy is what, $45? That should hold all the fake pics of Anna Kournikova's titties you could ever rub out to . . .

Funded with $14.6 million, MySpace.com employed around thirty people and went out of business in May 2001—giving customers a three-day notice to download their files before they were permanently deleted.

CYBERREBATE.COM

I've got a WHOLE BUNCH of electronics and crap here in my apartment. SEND ME MONEY, I'LL SEND YOU SOME CRAP. FILL OUT SOME FORMS, and then some time in the distant future I'll SEND YOU YOUR MONEY BACK.

Cool? Right on.

Welcome to CyberRebate.com, one of the biggest scams on the Internet. I shit you not, this company gave away stuff like Nintendo Game Boys, DVDs, and other products 100% free of charge.

Well sort of.

Customers had to actually buy the products at inflated prices (like $150 for one DVD) and then fourteen weeks later, CyberRebate would send the customer a check for the purchase price.

Well sort of.

So many customers complained of never receiving their rebates that the Better Business Bureau gave CyberRebate its lowest rating—unsatisfactory. New York's attorney general launched an investigation. CyberRebate basically said, "Okay we really, really promise to start paying people on time," and everything was okay.

Well sort of.

Sounds like a Ponzi scheme, right? In other words . . . each rebate was paid for by the previous customer's purchase. And there's a fourteen-week buffer, so in the meanwhile, CyberRebate could invest their money in some red-hot (ha) tech stocks.

Customers who got in on the ground floor, and got out quick, did okay and got some shit for free. Those who stuck around to watch the thing crumble around them—they didn't do so well—at the time of bankruptcy, CyberRebate .com owed around $59 million to customers who were expecting rebates.

At one point, CyberRebate was said to be the third most frequented shopping site on the Web. A lot of their customers were people who couldn't afford stuff but had credit cards. They'd "buy" things from CyberRebate and just wait for their rebate. When the company declared bankruptcy, so did many of these customers.

In an example of pure fuckitude, one of CyberRebate's customers (and now one of CyberRebate's "20 largest creditors") was reportedly owed $115,000 in rebates. Apparently he used CyberRebate to basically get stuff for free and then resell it on eBay. Just the simple fact that this actually makes some kind of SENSE should get your spidey-sense tingling.

CyberRebate's customers couldn't dispute their credit-card charges because the Federal Trade Commission's regulations require consumers to dispute bad credit-card charges within nine weeks—CyberRebate had people believing that they'd get their rebates in fourteen.

So why aren't the founders in jail? They claimed that the way they were expecting to make money is from people *forgetting* to fill out the rebate forms. So . . . basically the business plan was to overcharge customers and then bet on their stupidity.

Well sort of.

DESKTOP.COM

Yet another "free hard drive" site, this one with the addition of a few applications you could run over the Internet. Don't get me wrong—one day it'll be nice to have pay-per-use software that I don't need to store locally on my computer. The way I see it, Desktop.com blew their $29 million funding building the environment, instead of building the software that would make customers want to use it.

The application service provider (ASP) acronym that's misused so often will eventually bring us back to thin clients or dumb terminals—cheap workstations that just need to connect to one another.

Look around your office—how many people really need to be using state-of-the-art Pentium IVs?

Well maybe that one guy who needs to shift between Word and the Quake tournament fast enough to keep his boss from getting a clue. Not possible at less than fifty frames a second . . .

Anyway . . . if a company wants to make money with this, they gotta *sell* something.

People who relied on Desktop.com just before the company went under experienced the ASP equivalent of a fatal disk crash. Glad I decided to do my computing on my computer, rather than trust my files and apps to another bubble-rider.

QUIT WHILE YOU'RE AHEAD

LIQUOR.COM

Way back in 1940, a chain of liquor stores called Foremost Liquor created a service called Foremost Liquor-by-Wire. The idea was simple—call a phone number, place an order, and have it delivered to you by your local Foremost Liquor store.

The business was passed down through the family, and fifty-one years later, Barry Grieff, grandson of the original founder, decided to run Liquor-by-Wire as an independent business and basically be the "FTD" of the liquor biz. For eight years, the business was run by only four people, and it was nicely profitable with $3 million in sales and 30% to 35% margins.

Fast-forward to 1999. They changed their name to Liquor.com, launched a site, got sucked into IPO madness, hired a bunch of suits to help them go public, and the rest is history . . . They went from four people and making a profit in 1999 as Liquor-by-Wire, to over forty people and losing their shirts in 2000 as Liquor.com.

HEAVENLYDOOR.COM

Biopharmaceutical company Procept-HD thought it would be a good idea to branch out into the dot-com biz. And so HeavenlyDoor.com was opened for business, a site selling caskets, flowers, and plots—a virtual Yellow Pages for burial-related businesses.

Procept-HD reported losing $25.9 million on the idea in just nine months before selling their web assets to rival RememberedOnes.com.

I personally had never heard of HeavenlyDoor until I reported their demise—but one of Fuckedcompany.com's message board users had some insight:

The problem was shipping.

I used HeavenlyDoor.com and set up "MyHeavenlyDoor." When Uncle Ed died last month, I packed him in a box and sent him off for a proper funeral. Actually, because of the 75-lb. weight restriction with UPS, I had to send 3 boxes. But still, off he went.

Two weeks later I get a return box from HeavenlyDoor saying that because they only received 1 of 3 boxes, they were returning it to me. What's up with that? It's poor customer service like that, that will kill a company. I'm not surprised they went under.

If anyone finds one or both of the missing boxes, email me. Thanks.

BUILDNET.COM

Witness the downward spiral that was BuildNet.com.

It was early 2000 . . . things were looking bright. Build-Net was already a successful developer of project management software for builders. Software to generate schedules, estimate purchase orders, work orders . . . They were kicking ass, their software was used to construct almost one-third of all new homes built in the United States.

They'd just received about $142 million funding to develop a website linking builders to a network of distributors and manufacturers. Just what the industry needed, they said.

With about 1,000 people on staff, the company basically pulled a dot-com and built yet another online shopping site, this one selling stuff for residential home builders. They had the IPO all planned out, papers filed in September 2000, set to raise $230 million more.

But the market . . .

So this led to that, and a few months later reality set in. BuildNet cheeses cancelled their public offering and laid off around 75% of their workforce. BuildNet's president resigned, I guess an admission that the company was in deep doo-doo.

But then good news!

In June 2001, competitor HomeSphere signed an agreement to purchase BuildNet for $35 million. Yeah BuildNet already spent almost $142 million on the disaster, but hey, any chance to offload the fucker was worth it. In the meanwhile, to save cash, remaining BuildNet employees were asked to take a mandatory, unpaid five-week vacation.

Uh-oh.

One month later, HomeSphere apparently wised up and pulled out of the deal. BuildNet filed Chapter 11 bankruptcy.

BuildNet's remaining assets were sold at auction for less than $5 million.

Sniff sniff.

ZAP.COM

Zapata Corporation was founded in 1953 as a contract offshore oil-drilling company. In the 1970s, they began making fish oil and sausage casings. Yes, I said fish oil and sausage casings. And in 1998 . . . they got into the Internet business. To the casual observer, it seemed as if their snappy domain name, Zap.com, was burning a hole in their pocket.

"Hey, people are making dough on the Internet, let's give it a shot. Portal, you say?"

And so they offered to acquire Excite.com for $1.68 billion and jump into the portal business. Excite rejected the offer, dismissing it as a publicity stunt. And also said something about how they didn't "synergize well" or some such hilarity.

So Zapata made its own stupid little portal, Zap.com. And then announced that they were taking it down.

A few months later, Zap.com came back to life, but this time as a content publisher. They arranged to buy a number of content sites, including Word.com, the classic e-zine founded in 1995. That idea didn't last too long either— Zapata killed the whole thing in January 2001, taking a $5.7 million hit for their nine-month dot-com stint.

Oh yeah, the original founder of Zapata back in 1953 was George Bush (senior)—who cashed out in the 1960s.

WINGSPAN BANK

Launched by Bank One in June 1999, Wingspan Bank was a pure, Internet-only bank.

Let's see . . . they paid higher interest than other banks, they charged no fees for practically any of their services, they refunded ATM fees from any bank's ATM machines, and they gave $100 free to their first 10,000 customers.

And they went BROKE!

Shocker.

Seems customers were happy with the service (why wouldn't they be?)—Wingspan just had a crappy business model that failed to include any real profit-making.

Around August 2001, it was announced that Wingspan customers would soon be Bank One customers. . . . . .

MEALS.COM

Before telling you what I know about Meals.com, I'll begin by telling you about their parent company, Coinstar. Coinstar makes those big ugly green contraptions at the grocery store that you see all those heehaws dumping jars of pennies into. The machines count change and dispense vouchers that can be traded in for cash.

Using their supermarket connections and their penchant for big ugly doohickeys, Coinstar developed Meals.com. Meals.com itself was a food portal (I can't believe I wrote "food portal") where users could log in and browse different products and recipes (see *FooDoo.com*). Said users would then sign up for and receive a Meals.com Card, which they could swipe at any Meals.com kiosk, which were to be located in grocery stores around the country. The kiosks would then dispense coupons targeted toward the shopper, as well as an itemized shopping list.

Revenue stream? Advertising inserts in the recipes, of course. 1 PACKAGE ORTEGA BRAND SUPER-DELUXE FLOUR TORTILLAS. Right, like that.

So . . . it was basically the equivalent of, say, FAXING YOUR SHOPPING LIST TO THE GROCERY STORE

AND PICKING IT UP THERE instead of just folding the thing and putting it in your pocket. Oh and they gave you coupons. Whoopee.

Meals.com had ninety employees, received $10 million from Coinstar and an additional $5.5 million from outside investors. After taking a huge loss, Coinstar gave up on the whole Meals.com kiosk thing, and as of this writing, Meals .com exists as but another online recipe file.

So like, tonight I'm having my usual dinner of Cocoa Krispies, but I'm having a guest soon. I need to know how much Cocoa Krispies and milk to buy for two. What will I do . . . what *will* I do?

MUSIC.COM

True story.

It was 1999 and I was a freelance programmer working from my one-bedroom apartment here in Midtown Manhattan. I'd just quit my job at a major web shop in pursuit of creating my own Internet consultancy that wasn't based on pure horse crap.

The phone rings. Some fucksteak on the other end is asking me how much I'd charge him to make a "music portal."

"Umm, don't you think there are enough music sites out there?" I asked.

"Yeah, but we're MUSIC.COM," he answered, as if he were "on to something."

Okay it was definitely cool that this dude had the "Music.com" domain name, so we started talking. Turns out he used to work for a Philippine semiconductor company. Specifically, Multi-User Specialty Integrated Circuits—M.U.S.I.C. In 1992 he registered the available and obvious domain name, Music.com.

So basically, the whole dot-com craze happened seven years later and M.U.S.I.C. thought they were sitting on a gold mine with this domain name. Put the semiconductor biz on the back burner, started yet another music site.

DAAAAAAAA!!

They were unfocused and did everything from selling CDs and musical instruments to an ever-stupid online cemetery where you could pay respects to dead rock stars.

Anyway, their name alone procured deals with big shots like Microsoft, DreamWorks, and Virgin. Still didn't matter—they lost $1.5 million the first year, shut it down, and continue to make semiconductors. Music.com now appears to be some half-assed site with links to other e-commerce sites.

I never got the job.

EXPRESS.COM

Pretty simple, really. Founded by the guy who produced *The A-Team* and *21 Jump Street*, Express.com started out in 1996 as DVDExpress.com. They were the first company to sell DVD movies online.

At the time they were founded, most people didn't even know what a DVD was. They were smart, got in early, and became the largest DVD retailer on the Web. It was especially brilliant because, for a long time, places like Blockbuster had tiny DVD selections—shopping for movies on the Web was perfect . . . not to mention their great PORNOGRAPHY selection.

But in 1999 they got cocky, became Express.com, and started selling music CDs. At that point the Web was already saturated with failing music retailers. It was hopeless. As if they weren't losing money fast enough, they then bought GameCave.com and started selling video games.

Finally, the powdered sugar on this ass-flavored funnel cake was buying the GameFan Network—an ad network and hosting service for gaming websites. Basically, they hosted small game-related websites (affiliates) and then attempted to sell ads for the affiliate sites, paying webmasters 50% of ad revenue.

Word on the street is that the Express.com-owned GameFan Network never paid their affiliates, but that's a different story . . .

Anyway, they started out great, built a nice community of DVD shoppers, and had $16 million in sales in 1998. Even so, they still managed to blow through at least $55 million in funding, hire and fire 230 people, vacate their 66,000-square-foot warehouse, and file Chapter 11.

Their remains were bought by a new company who changed it back to DVDExpress.com and relaunched the site.

WORK.COM

The idea, of course, was to take it public and cash out with millions.

Backed by Dow Jones and Excite and employing over 100 unlucky people, Work.com offered news, stocks, and everything else one could find on any of the thousands of "portals" on the Web.

You'd think that Dow Jones, Work.com backer and publisher of *The Wall Street Journal*, would have read its own reports . . . Work.com launched in April 2000, right when the public woke up to IPO scams like this.

In another brilliant move, Business.com, which paid $7.5 million for their own domain name, bought Work.com's domain name after Work.com folded.

TOYSRUS.COM

In December 1999, basically every online retailer promised that they could ship in time for Christmas. In July 2000, the FTC fined ToysRUs.com, along with three other online retailers, $1.5 million for breaking that promise.

ToysRUs.com was also an example of how faulty technology can kill a dot-com business. The custom application Toys "R" Us commissioned to run their site was buggy, slow, and often broken, despite the fact that the site was purportedly powered by over 250 individual web servers.

About three months before the 2000 holiday season, Toys "R" Us abandoned their troublesome website and turned sales over to Amazon.com as part of a ten-year agreement.

FINANCE.COM

Even Citibank can fuck it up.

The slogan for their little-known financial services dotcom venture, Finance.com, was *"Just Money, No Rocket Science."* At least they hit half their mark.

Had their motto been "No money, no rocket science," they'd be batting a thousand . . .

BALDUCCI.COM

Balducci's is a successful retailer of gourmet groceries and prepared foods, having been in business since 1946. Hoping to cash in on that crazy "Internet" thing, they dropped a ton of dough and started an e-commerce site.

First, let me say that online grocery delivery may be unwieldy (see *Webvan*), but it's definitely handy. If you're cooking for a large dinner party, it really sucks having to move thirty bags of groceries from the store to your car to your home—not to mention if you live in a carless town like New York City.

Not that I've ever cooked for a large dinner party. Or a small one. Or really anything. But yeah.

A large percentage of Balducci's products are perishable. Big orders cause shipping delays, and well, if a DVD gets delivered late, no problem. When the same thing happens with a frozen steak, you're fucked—as were many of their customers before they shut the dot-com down.

DAILYRADAR.COM

Future Net, the British publishing company that publishes the craptacular new economy magazine *Business 2.0,* has a U.S. subsidiary called Imagine Media. As the publisher of offline magazines *Mac Addict* and *PC Gamer,* Imagine Media made the right move when they closed down their popular gaming site, DailyRadar.com.

In an email to its two dozen employees, management said that the closure was due to the fact that DailyRadar wasn't on track to reach profitability *fast enough*, which of course insinuates that they thought they could have actually made a buck off this one in the long run.

Not bloody likely.

Furthermore, DailyRadar.com, which consisted mainly of video game and console reviews and articles, perhaps competed with Imagine's flagship, long running, and assumed profitable offline magazine, *PC Gamer*. My guess is Imagine realized that it wasn't such a good idea to create a practically revenue-less dot-bomb to perhaps compete with their flagship, money-making offline magazine.

I think Imagine Media's big mistake was folding their magazine *PC Accelerator* into DailyRadar.com before closing the whole thing. *PC Accelerator* was kind of *PC Gamer* meets *Maxim* meets *Hustler*. I don't really play computer games, much less read about them . . . but with detailed reviews of Tomb Raider Lara Croft's huge digital boobies, even *I* saw the value . . .

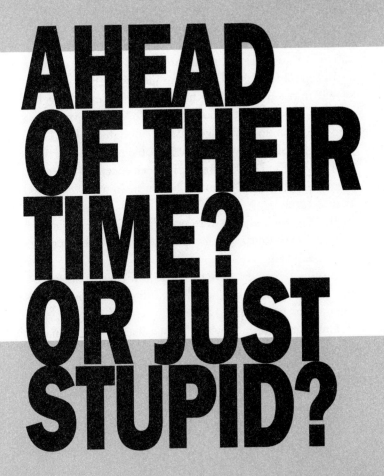

AHEAD OF THEIR TIME? OR JUST STUPID?

Z.COM

Another winner backed by incubator idealab!^{SM}, Z.com developed original programming for the Internet.

Broadband, fast shared Internet connections, are cool and relatively cheap. I'm still a believer in the convergence of TV and Internet. Personally, I listen to more Internet radio than I do terrestrial radio, and that's a start.

But simply put, 1999/2000 was just too early to sink a lot of $$$ into something like this. Being first is one thing, but when you've only got enough money to last for a year or so and the technology isn't widespread enough to SUPPORT YOUR BUSINESS, you've got a problem.

TV, VCR, DVD, movie theaters, peep-show spank booths . . . there are so many better ways to watch video than Z.com.

Besides, their shows were crap. Their comedy channel was not at all funny, despite the efforts of comedy powerhouse Bob Saget . . . ugh.

Although they did have this one show called *Dare for Dollars*. They had stuff like hot chicks riding rodeo bulls wearing nothing but whipped cream.

Could it make money? No. But I liked watching naked chicks bouncing around on rodeo bulls.

Toss My Salad

Z.com might have had a chance if their plan to have comedian Chris Rock help develop content ever happened. Instead, they went into negotiations and paid Rock over $1 million that was supposed to be returned if a deal hadn't surfaced after thirty days.

News of the pending deal hit the wires and Z.com had the advantage of being associated with Chris Rock.

Then the deal fell through. Z.com asked for their money back. First nicely, and then they sued Rock.

Rock later countersued, essentially claiming that Z.com obfuscated things and delayed the deal-making process, hence benefiting from Rock's name for free.

He was also promised Z.com stock and was pissed that he got taken in a dot-scam.

The suits were eventually dropped and the matter was resolved out of court.

WAPIT.COM

The founder of Wapit, Mato Valtonen, was apparently some weird Finnish rock star or something. I dunno . . . Google it.

Anyway, if you don't know, WAP stands for wireless application protocol. It's the standard for wireless Internet data communication, equivalent to HTTP for web browsing and FTP for transferring files.

Wapit was both a portal for wireless Internet devices (a.k.a. cell phones) but gained more notoriety as a maker of WAP-related software. In particular, Wapit developed Kannel, a WAP gateway (Apache for WAP, for the dorks in the house).

Wapit also created imbedded software—software that's built into your wireless device that works with wireless Internet services. They even scored a distribution deal with Nokia at one point. The problem is that practically as soon as these devices are released, they're already obsolete and replaced.

Whether they were brilliant and ahead of their time, or whether they were just a bunch of fucknozzles, wireless Internet technology at the time certainly wasn't ready for a multimillion-dollar wireless middleware company . . . I mean, playing Tetris or even checking a movie listing on your cell phone's 160 X 120 display might be a hoot for a whole five minutes, but then the novelty is over.

Receiving first-round funding of $2 million and employing around 100 people, they were counting on that elusive second round—which never happened.

The company had a cool name though. I love to wapit in

the morning when I first wake up with my stiffy, wapit in the stall of the men's room at lunchtime, and wapit before I go to sleep.

THAT, is true. And THAT is why you bought this book.

MVP.COM

With $65 million funding by sports legends Michael Jordan, Wayne Gretzky, John Elway, and others, MVP.com has proven my theory that fame and wealth not only corrupt, but also lower one's intelligence.

You become a football or basketball star and think that just because you dominate in one field, you're automatically gifted in fields you've no right to be in. Celebrity restaurants? Car dealerships? Websites? "The Magic Hour"?

Please.

Like fucking jocks even went to class. Yes, I see the irony of a programmer writing a book. Shut up now.

MVP.com, which at one point employed over 160 people, sold sporting goods at inflated prices. No lie. The premise of their business plan was that people would pay extra for this stuff because of the three famous investors.

On one hand, I think they kinda had the right idea—finally an e-commerce site that didn't sell *below* cost. Still, people were unwilling to pay extra on top of having to wait for the delivery.

In their last breath, MVP.com sold their domain name and customer database—but not their famous investors—to former partner CBS Sportsline, who's trying to give it another go . . .

GLOBALMEDIA.COM

GlobalMedia.com started off providing streaming services for regular, terrestrial (ya know, AM/FM) radio stations. There are many legal and business implications involved in streaming a radio station over the Internet. For example, do advertisers pay more? Do advertisers *want* their ads from one market to play in another market? What about syndicated on-air personalities—will their shows be bought in other markets now that people can just pick 'em up on the Web?

Probably due to these and other problems, GlobalMedia left the terrestrial radio business and focused on basically providing just another Internet-only radio station. Hey I like Internet radio, but I like it because it's commercial free. Other than that, the sound quality sucks and it's a pain in the ass.

Yeah yeah one day we'll all be listening to digital radio (companies like XM and Serius are working on it). Someday we'll be doing a lot of stuff. There's one thing that people won't be doing someday, though: working at GlobalMedia.

The company laid off 120 people and reported a more than $15 million net loss for the second quarter of fiscal 2001.

MYBIZ.COM

When dot-coms really started biting the dust at an alarming rate (around April 2000), everyone had a different explanation for what went wrong. A popular one was lack of customer service. I don't buy it—I mean, when you go to the local bookstore, how often do you need any customer service above maybe asking if a particular book is in stock?

Regardless, the end of the dot-com boom saw the beginning of the customer relationship management (eCRM) boom. Many companies claimed that their eCRM solutions were the holy grail. One such company was MyBiz .com.

Funded by Idealab, the same jokers who brought us eToys.com, Eve.com, and Utility.com, MyBiz.com helped small- to medium-size businesses track their customers, build mailing lists, and spam them.

Luckily it didn't get too big—employing twelve people, MyBiz.com lasted just nine months from launch to dot-com graveyard.

RX.COM

Online drugstore Rx.com claimed to be different than their many competitors (including Soma.com, Drugstore.com, PlanetRX.com, and even Walgreens.com) in that Rx.com was targeting big institutional buyers, saying it wasn't cost effective to go after the individual consumer. Yet of their over $350 million in venture capital, $37.5 million came in the form of advertising and promotion from television network CBS, and $25 million went to Austin's The Think Tank advertising agency for a one-year stint.

Regardless, Rx.com was a classic example of how technology can really fuck shit up. This company had $350 million to build a fucking website and market it a little. I mean, if they spent $1 million a year, they could have been around for hundreds of years without a single sale.

But no, they had to build a wildly complicated, incredibly expensive beast of a web application. All this technology and equipment was of course maintained by a highly paid staff and a wasteful and excessive management team.

The best part of this shit sandwich is that once it was up and running, nobody wanted to come take a bite. Well I guess a few did out of novelty, but the mad geriatric online rush of prescriptions that was supposed to happen, never did.

Word is that Rx.com's employees couldn't even order prescriptions from Rx.com with their own Rx.com insurance. That should have been a sign—if their own employees couldn't buy from Rx.com, who was supposed to?

BROADBAND OFFICE

Broadband Office tried to sell high-speed Internet access to people. They blamed the market for their closure.

THE MARKET? People jump through HOOPS to get broadband access. The market was hungry.

They had a reported $250 million in venture capital funding. They had the former commissioner of the FCC on board. They had strong relationships with eight of the country's largest real-estate companies, giving them access to 20% of the nation's commercial office space. They had a network built by a former director of UUNet. They had millions in backing by rival companies Microsoft *and* Sun Microsystems, giving them access to all sorts of crazy silly technology. They had over 700 dedicated employees. They were supposedly valued at $1.5 billion.

Yet they failed. Employees blamed incompetent management, pointing fingers at the twenty-something CEO who had little experience. I blame growing to 700 employees in eight months, with little to no revenue. I blame execs looking forward to their exit strategies. I blame the company for being overly concerned with being the "next big, cool thing," rather than trying to figure out how to be a successful business.

Provide the service when the demand is there, grow as you need to, charge more than it costs you, you'll survive.

Employees were laid off with no warning and received no severance pay. An email sent to employees stated that their last week's salary, vacation, and business expenses would be handled by bankruptcy court.

HITPLAY MEDIA

In early 1999, an excited executive at the NBC television network brought an idea to the table—an online television network. NBC wasn't interested. So he quit and started his own online television network, Hitplay Media.

The site, Hitplay.com, was essentially just another site that streamed video. Their content included reruns of sixties and seventies game shows. Woohoo.

Despite the obvious lack of *entertainment*, and despite the fact that Blues Brothers Dan Aykroyd and Jim Belushi were on board (okay . . . *almost* the Blues Brothers), nobody was interested.

Why?

Let's figure it out.

Why is the Web, as a medium, cool? Because of hyperlinks, plain and simple. Nothing can compete with the Web in that respect. Not TV, not radio, not a book.

In 1999, high-quality streaming video wasn't happening. Almost everyone was using a modem, online videos were little three-inch choppy squares. TV won that battle, done.

"But look at the numbers!" they said. Video streaming over the Internet grows over 200% yearly. Over 33 million people watch streamed video monthly. It's estimated that 89% of all websites will offer streaming media within two years.

Right.

Of course, eventually, once everyone's Internet connections are fast and everyone's got the hardware to handle it, we'll all be watching *Regis* on the Internet. It's already happening, sort of, with digital cable TV. But in 1999, with only enough cash to last for a couple of years, there's no way this was gonna happen.

So anyway . . . one semicool thing came out of it . . . a technology for inserting targeted video ads in Internet video streams. Again, definitely before their time—but so before their time it was stupid. Like opening a store that sells space suits and wondering why nobody's buying . . . or something.

Regardless, they totally switched gears, ceased trying to make it as an online TV network, and became an ASP focusing on "Cupid"—their ad-insertion service.

That didn't last long either—over $8 million and thirty-five people were burned.

Far as I know, NBC is still in business and doing fine . . . ya know?

LIPSTREAM.COM

LipStream was another voice-over-IP (VoIP) company (see *Multitude.com*). VoIP means essentially using your computer as a telephone, and using the Internet and the vendor (LipStream) as the telephone company.

Before I get started here, let me state that already, so much of our telephone communications are based on digital networks that I'm certain we're all gonna be using VoIP eventually . . . the problem is, when this company started in 1999, starting a phone vs. VoIP battle was stupid.

To get VoIP to work properly, you needed all your hardware to work just right—sound card, speakers, microphone . . . much easier to just pick up the trusty old telephone handset. Also, VoIP service was inconsistent and the sound quality *at best* was that of a cell phone. I played around with VoIP a few times and often the conversations were so garbled and lagged that I just gave up. Again, this will all be taken care of once everyone's bandwidth and 'puter can handle it—we just ain't there yet.

Funded with over $22 million and employing around eighty-five people, LipStream's target customers included websites that wanted to provide live customer support. IF YER GONNA TALK, PICK UP THE DAMN PHONE.

LipStream's mission was basically to build this semicool technology that nobody needed or wanted and then to try to trick people into thinking that it's better than the telephone.

PROMPTU

One phenomenon of the early dot-com days was that non-techies were SO DAMN IMPRESSED by every little doo-hickey, animated graphic, and dynamic content page. As a techie, it was pretty easy to get people to throw money your way with very little effort.

Promptu was one such example, except they only succeeded in squeezing money from investors—not customers. Promptu developed an extranet designed for enabling communication between a company's marketing and sales departments. For you dingleberries who don't know, an extranet is a website that's for internal, corporate use only, but is accessible from anywhere by authorized users.

Anyway, a common customer testimonial for Promptu's product was usually along the lines of: "BEFORE Promptu, if we wanted to share information via the Web, we had to build websites from SCRATCH! It took WEEKS just to get an image online for everyone to look at. But NOWWW with PROMPTU . . . we simply click a button and there it is!"

Not so impressed.

Making matters worse, Promptu informed customers that it was not unusual for their software to take eight to twelve WEEKS just to get up and running. Must I mention that Promptu's service cost over $100,000 annually, with implementation sometimes costing up to $75,000?

With hardly any customers, Promptu managed to burn through over $24 million in funding.

NETMORF

NetMorf spent about $11 million making a product called SiteMorfer. Basically, it was a wireless application protocol (WAP) server that could transform existing online information into a format that could be viewed on wireless devices like cell phones and PDAs.

Eventually, such a product will be a necessity for commercial websites. Personally, I think Microsoft will make a version and bundle it for "free" with Internet Information Server (IIS), their somewhat ubiquitous web/FTP server, crushing all competition. But that's a different book.

Anyway, in the late-nineties and early 2000s, wireless usage was not nearly popular enough to keep any company like this in business. It's not fast enough, the screens are tiny, it's too expensive, and honestly, how many times are you *really* far enough from a computer that you *need* to surf RIGHT NOW?

Unless they had the millions upon millions to burn while waiting a few years for people to start using wireless Internet, they were doomed for failure.

Which they apparently were.

And they called it "m-business," for *mobile* business. When I hear this, I think of Mr. Garrison saying "m-kay?" Whoever started calling it m-business should be m-slapped around.

URBAN COOL NETWORK

Urban Cool Network consisted of two things. First was a website targeted toward minorities ("urban," in politically correct marketing speak). It consisted of the same old news, entertainment, and shopping that one could expect from any of the thousands of similar sites.

The thing that made Urban Cool Network stand out was that they were also building physical kiosks and putting them in high-traffic, primarily urban areas. Used like public phone booths, the kiosks were hooked up with high-speed Internet access.

Of course, the Internet kiosks would have been FREE to use.

A few things here. First, it's naïve to think that an "urban" site's target audience is made up of minorities. The more urban-popular something is, the more popular it will become with suburban white kids (and . . . twenty-five-year-old New York City Jewish kids who are rockin out to Snoop Dogg as we speak).

So . . . nothing inherently wrong with that—consumers are consumers. The problem was that Urban Cool Network started believing themselves, and started putting their kiosks in primarily minority areas.

Being as they were planning on making money from advertising and affiliate shopping links, the company would have fared better by putting their kiosks in shopping malls in Toledo.

Or maybe outside Hebrew schools in Manhattan.

Second. They thought it was advantageous from both a business as well as a social standpoint to get minorities online by showing them how neat-o high-speed Internet access can be. And they were right; it certainly is neat-o.

But they thought their users could be easily led. They were wrong. That really goes for *anything* marketed toward young people. We hate being marketed to. It's hard to trick us into buying your crap.

Not to mention that maintaining thousands of public Internet terminals would be a complete nightmare. Think about how big the help desk/tech support department is at a 10,000-person company. Now imagine supporting 200,000 public computers, all over the country.

Had Urban Cool Network actually gone public (which they were on the verge of doing) and their ideas become reality, maintaining the kiosks would have put them out of business.

MUSICMAKER.COM

MusicMaker let customers pick songs and build customized CDs for 10 bucks a pop.

The first year of their existence, this company grossed $74,028 in sales. The next year, they went public and miraculously raised $117.6 million—with music giant EMI as their largest shareholder.

One of the problems MusicMaker had was that, expectedly, they couldn't get licenses for a lot of the music that people wanted. It looked as if EMI was thinking, "Hey, people will just be able to buy our music, cool!"—but they weren't thinking about the startup they were helping to build.

EMI probably figured that even if the thing failed, which it did of course, maybe they'd have sold enough music to at least have broken even. But with MusicMaker's limited catalog, it never caught on.

And of course, most importantly, MusicMaker couldn't

compete against companies like Napster, who at the time were giving it away for free.

When they received notice from Nasdaq that their stock was about to be delisted, MusicMaker did what was to become a dot-com tradition—the 1-for-10 *reverse* stock split, generally enacted to bring the stock's price just above Nasdaq's minimum of $1.

ANTEYE.COM

Launched right around the same time that I started Fuckedcompany.com, AntEye.com existed as a means to accept submissions from amateur filmmakers, let users vote on the films, and offer development deals to the most popular. Pilots would be produced with a 50-50 deal between AntEye.com and the filmmaker, should it be sold to a network or studio.

Not a terrible idea, but to basically 99% of the people who visited the site, it appeared to be one of the thousands of broadband short-film broadcasters already in business. And well . . . I've been dragged to enough amateur student film shows in college to know that they are mostly krapity krap krap krap. Cute artsy chicks tho.

Anyway, they also had about five years to go before 0.00001% of the population had the required technology, broadband, whatever, needed to view the things in full splendor.

With less money than most, they took a bunch of egoists with little experience in their industry, made them into a company, and gave paychecks they could have only dreamt of . . .

MP3.com invested $4 million into AntEye.com, which folded only eight months later in December 2000.

XUMA.COM

Another managed services company (see *LogicTier* for details), Xuma.com tried to differentiate themselves from the herd by marketing SPEED SPEED SPEED, FIRST MOVER ADVANTAGE! "We'll build you an entire network and website in ONE FUCKING DAY YOU SHITHOSES!!" was basically their mantra. Except for the "shithoses" part.

Hey I never said that managed services were a bad idea—I use a managed services firm to host Fuckedcompany.com—but many (LoudCloud, LogicTier, and Xuma to name a few) were destined for the pages of this book.

"Why?" you ask.

Their clients were dying fast—they didn't need e-business solutions, they needed CUSTOMERS.

So let's recap: CEO leaves, employees get pink slips, investors get zip, Cisco and Sun make assloads of money selling them crap.

$48 million lost and over 300 employees forced to work on their résumés.

CONTENT WAS KING

RIVALS.COM

I think the elevator pitch to investors went something like this: "Oh yeah, that's how we'll make money—a sports site. Really, there will be lots of tie-ins. We can sell, umm, T-shirts. And banner ads. And, umm, here, I'm thinking, umm, we could make like a 'premium content' section. But it would be hard to charge for it, so we could give it away for free for a while. Yeah, after that we could make money . . . doing something, well, shit. Never mind. Can I have $75 million?"

And thus $75 million was granted to sports site Rivals .com, making it one of the most heavily financed Internet companies in Seattle.

Sports content just could not generate revenue. Just ask Rivals.com, Quokka (see *"Torched,"* p. 57), Broadband Sports, MVP.com (see p. 79), the list goes on . . .

They never figured out how to make money. At one point, Rivals.com was bloated with 150 employees, burning $2 million per month. The company was clearly gunning for the "hurry-up-and-IPO-and-fucking-cash-out-quick-before-anyone-finds-out" strategy. In March 2000, they even filed for a $100 million IPO.

Right, like that was gonna happen.

Instead, money was running out. They tried to sell but nobody was buying. They even announced that an acquisition was in the works with Yahoo!, but it never happened. They started winding down by canning ad sales people and outsourcing ad sales to a company called Phase2Media—a fellow Fuckedcompany.com Hall-of-Famer.

Money was so tight that before Rivals.com closed up

Shaddup

Sometimes laid-off employees have to sign a contract in order to receive severance pay. Rivals.com had one of the heftier severance contracts, which included a "non-disparagement" clause.

Aching for his two-week check, one former Rivals.com employee told WashTech.com, "What exactly is 'disparaging' anyway? Who determines that? Is it disparaging to say that Rival Networks was incapable of taking 1.3 million unique monthly visitors to its website and making any profit off that?"

Hope not, cuz you just did.

shop in April 2001, they even considered selling the $5 million in advertising they were entitled to on Foxsports.com (News Corp. was a major investor) to other sites.

BUT HEY, THEY HAD 20 MILLION PAGEVIEWS A DAY! Douchebags.

In an odd twist of fate, one of the companies that Rivals .com bought for $2.5 million back in the day, Alliance-Sports, bought Rival.com's assets for "pennies on the dollar" after Rivals.com shut down. Right on!

CONTENTVILLE.COM

Founded in July 2000, ContentVille.com charged users to download digital books, term papers, speeches, and other content. They later (supposedly unwittingly) became the Napster of print.

Here's how it worked: Users went to ContentVille.com and typed any subject in the site's "search" box. The site would return a list of matching documents, which, for a fee, could be downloaded. Besides the fact that these fuckmustards spent a reported $40 million on advertising, they had another problem on their hands.

Writers and scholars started finding that their own works were for sale on the site—without their knowledge or permission.

That pissed off authors.

Also, some of the content available for sale on the site could be obtained for free from originating sites. For example, *Village Voice* articles: These articles were available for pay on ContentVille.com—or for free on VillageVoice.com.

That pissed off users.

So everyone pretty much hated the service, even though founder Steve Brill (founder, *The American Lawyer* magazine, Court TV) claimed that he legitimately purchased the rights to the content from other content providers (who supposedly purchased them from colleges).

The company tried to patch things up . . . removed articles like those from the *Village Voice* . . . tried to funnel royalties to authors . . . gave up and in October 2001 left ContentVille.com a ghost town.

NEXT50.COM

The shutdown notice on Next50.com's site read (in

BIG BIG LETTERS SO

EVEN OLD PEOPLE COULD READ IT), *"We were well on our way to creating THE Internet resource for folks over 50."*

Like that's something to aspire to?

So yeah old people control all the money . . . point taken. But they don't use the Internet. And I'm not generalizing. People over fifty DO NOT use the Web.

Honest.

"Where's the 'any' key? I hate this damn Interweb. And I just shit myself. Again."

I dunno . . . they were yet another content site, offering articles about this, that, and the other thing . . . you know the drill. They thought they were gonna make money by re-selling some lame ISP service and by tricking old people into signing up for "opt-in" spam networks.

(For all the people over fifty reading this . . . ha ha I'm just kidding, I know you use the Web. Now knit me some mittens.)

Next50's parent company, "DWC Web Corp.," reportedly raised $3 million. Not sure how much of that went into their Next50 masterpiece. Probably much.

HOOKT.COM

Despite their clever misspelling of the word "hooked" and their gratuitous use of Flash animation, Hookt.com was just another hip-hop corporation trying to cash in on hip-hop's bling-bling excessive spending (see *Urban Box Office*).

"The man is keeping us down! Check here to save 10% on a $250 Pelle Pelle sweater."

\<rant\>

Hip-hop started out as an underground movement. Record companies, MTV, and Puff Daddy (who incidentally was an investor in Hookt.com) changed all that. They popped it up and brought hip-hop to the mainstream. They generated tons of money at the expense of alienating old school hip-hoppers and tarnishing their culture.

With the Web is an opportunity for a second hip-hop renaissance. Underground art, music, and culture proliferate online. Check it out and . . . "keep it real!" As the kids say.

Word to your momma's uncle.

\</rant\>

Funded with almost $20 million, Hookt.com declared bankruptcy in May 2001.

LOCALBUSINESS.COM

This one made me kinda sad cuz they were a relatively big advertiser on Fuckedcompany.com. (No, it wasn't my fault they went under . . . blah.)

As their name suggests, LocalBusiness.com was an on-line news resource covering small- and medium-size business news in twenty-eight metropolitan areas. They also had message boards and all the other underutilized-but-requisite community stuff.

A lot of news sites like LocalBusiness.com—and there are a million of 'em—are accused of pretty much regurgitating press releases. This might be true, but I personally found them to be one of the best news sites out there . . . Shit, I used to just copy their crap (along with shit from CNET's News.com . . . gotta give 'em props, yo) and paste it into Fuckedcompany.

Actually, no I didn't. No really. No.

Actually, I'm convinced that in their later months they started copying shit from *me* . . .

Anyway, I was saying.

They had a plan for spending money, but not a plan for earning it. A big content site like LocalBusiness.com is one of the most expensive websites you can build. Sites like these take advantage of the large audience that is the Internet, but can't really benefit so much from computer technology and automation—a human still has to write each story.

And the company was reliant upon advertising for revenues, and we all know how that goes . . . Actually, that's not entirely true—at one point they acquired a company called TrueAdvantage. TrueAdvantage, which as of this writing still exists, is a business-intelligence gatherer. They acquire request for proposals (RFPs) and boast having RFPs for over $1 billion worth of work. The weird part is that, *that* actually sounds like a viable business . . .

Anyway, business plan or not, many were sad to see

LocalBusiness.com go. They were a relatively good, quick read on the local market. In a normal world they could have made it by charging for subscriptions. Of course, in the altered universe of the fucked dot-com, there are a million free news sites. One charges a subscription? Read another . . .

Same shit different URL.

LocalBusiness.com was initially funded with $16 million. The most the company ever generated in one year was $2 to $3 million. At its peak of foolishness, it employed around 125 people, 75 of whom were full-time journalists. After writing a reported 48,000 original stories, they filed Chapter 11 with just over $2.5 million in assets—and $1.5 million in liabilities.

Their assets were later bought at a public auction by the founders of TrueAdvantage—the company they had once acquired.

ETOWN.COM

Electronics retailer Best Buy sank $22 million into eTown .com, a site for consumer electronics reviews and product comparisons.

Yes, basically an online *Consumer Reports*. And yes, there were quite a number of other sites that did the same thing, and like eTown, didn't charge anything for their services. Best Buy's hope was that the site would push enough buyers to Best Buy so that it would be worth the investment.

They were wrong, it didn't.

Local 69

eTown.com was poised to be the first unionized dot-com.

Fed up with questionable job security and long hours, 70% of eTown's customer-service reps petitioned the National Labor Relations Board (NLRB) and were approved, thus making them the first dot-com to vote on whether or not to unionize.

Critics agreed that unions, which serve to make the workplace more fair by pretty much treating all employees the same whether they are slackers or performers, goes against the "new economy" environment that rewards innovation and originality.

Didn't matter though—eTown went out of business just before the vote happened.

IUMA.COM

Here's a lesson in how to fuck up a promising young company.

The Internet Underground Music Archive (IUMA.com) started in 1993, the same year that the Mosaic web browser was released. The site began the way it's *supposed* to begin—

a couple of college students started a small website to promote their own band and their friends' bands.

Soon IUMA became the largest community of unsigned bands and the first major electronic distribution site. Each band had a custom website where they could post music samples, sell CDs, and create message boards. Everything was peachy.

In June 1999, the inevitable happened. Fucked online music company eMusic.com bought them, pumped them full of money, and turned IUMA into just another big, ugly, overstaffed, profitless dot-com.

Putting the "FUN" in Dysfunctional!

In August 2000, IUMA started a promotion in which couples that named their babies "IUMA" would win a $5,000 cash prize.

To qualify, eligible parents had to register on the site and send a picture of the lucky kid with his/her birth certificate to IUMA.

The first human advertisement of a near-bankrupt dot-com company, Iuma Carlton, was born September 8, 2000, in St. Petersburg, Florida.

"It was easier than playing Lotto," said Dad.

It took about a year and a half for eMusic to realize their bad move, at which point IUMA's funding stopped, essentially pulling the rug out from under them. The whole thing crumbled, and on February 7, 2001, IUMA informed members that they had eliminated their entire staff.

In March 2001, a company called Vitaminic bought IUMA's remaining assets for $400,000 in cash and $500,000 in "stock" and relaunched the site complete with a new pay subscription service. We shall see . . .

VOTER.COM

Every person involved with founding or funding Voter.com should be imprisoned. The people who were paid the least should have the nicest cells, leaving VPs and CEOs in squalid, solitary shit pits, cramped and with poor ventilation.

And they had the gall to blame "market conditions."

The market could *not* have been better—the 2000 presidential election was arguably the most exciting in history, and was certainly the most watched. What better time for Voter.com, a site dedicated to political opinion and information, to make its mark. Millions of people turned to the Internet for real-time election news.

Problem was, the information Voter.com provided was available from a million other places . . . and honestly, most people don't really care about politics.

Despite the fact that Voter.com had absolutely no fucking business plan whatsoever, they still managed to employ 100 people (doing what, I have no idea) and burn over $20 million.

When they finally went out of business, these scumbags sold off (to multiple buyers) their user list of 170,000 email addresses, complete with personal information, including party affiliations and issues of interest.

Veto.

THE INDUSTRY STANDARD

Launched in 1997, *The Industry Standard* was one of the many "new economy" (no such thing) magazines to hit the market. It competed with *Fast Company, Business 2.0, eCompany Now, Upside, Red Herring,* and even *Wired.* As people started to figure out that the "new economy" (eyeballs! synergy! flooz!) was a joke, these magazines became kinda funny.

In January 2000, *The Industry Standard* raised $30 million from investors. It was right before the dot-com crash, so things were looking great. More like a phone book than a weekly magazine, each issue was around 300 pages.

Which leads me to PUD'S OFF-TOPIC YET HELPFUL TIP: Next time you're at the airport or wherever and you're about to stuff a bunch of magazines into your carry-on, wait! First flip through 'em and rip out each page that has an ad on both sides. You'll have much less magazine, plus it's FUN and EDUCATIONAL! Or not. Blah.

As I was saying . . .

Most of the ads in *The Industry Standard* seemed to be from investment banking firms, venture capital firms, and dot-coms. Mostly dot-coms. "We have the most ad pages of any publication on the planet," *The Standard*'s publisher told *Business Week*. Most of *The Standard*'s readers were dot-commers. Why were dot-coms advertising to one another? Methinks they were really advertising to venture capitalists. But we all know most VCs are clueless and don't read industry rags . . . right?

So fast-forward a few months . . . dot-coms crumbling, *Industry Standard* shrinking . . . 300 pages . . . 250 pages . . . 150 pages . . . 80 pages at the end.

Add on top of that the extravagance that was so popular amongst dot-coms at the time . . . *Industry Standard* wasn't immune. They hosted weekly rooftop parties in San Francisco and sponsored many an industry conference, including one in Barcelona where they reportedly dropped $1.4 million throwing a party.

As usual, I wasn't invited.

EVERYTHING THAT CAN BE DIGITAL, WILL BE— BUT SHOULDN'T BE

WINE.COM

I never got it.

I go to a party and have to bring wine, I can't wait a week (Wine.com's average shipping time), so I buy it at a store. I'm home alone, dick in hand, bottle of lube, and I feel like getting hammered, I go to the store for the cheap shit. I'm feeling like building a cellar? I buy on the advice of friends, sommeliers, and/or somebody who runs a fine liquor store.

Where does Wine.com fit in? How were they planning to make back their $200 million investment while earning a profit? (Hint: They weren't. My guess—they were planning to IPO or sell, cash out, and move to Barbados.)

An online wine venture on the national level is extremely difficult, if not impossible, due to liquor laws dating back to Prohibition—they couldn't ship to much of the country.

. . . not to mention breakable glass bottles . . .

It all comes down to the fact that efficient logistics separate the men from the boys—waiting a week for wine ain't gonna do it. Probably consuming too much of their own product, investors put $80 million into this company.

Pint-sized competitor eVineyard.com, later bought Wine .com's remaining assets for less than a reported $10 million.

EPPRAISALS.COM

I'm no expert in antiques (okay actually I'm an idiot) but I figure you need to actually SEE an antique to give it a proper appraisal.

No?

Gimme a copy of Photoshop and I'll show you a picture of my $4,000 "Ming vase."

Online antique appraisal company Eppraisals.com got off to a good start when they partnered with eBay.com, appraising antiques for the auction site. Apparently Eppraisals.com also contracted to independent appraisers and took a cut of the action. So like, this basically could have been a website with a bunch of appraisers' phone numbers.

Like there are so many people who need antiques appraised anyway.

\<angry pud\>

And if there's one thing I hate more than cocky, lying dot-com CEOs with blue shirts and Dockers, it's those little antique dealers with their bullshit glasses on a piece of cord shtick. What the fuck is that all about?

\</angry pud\>

Investors originally gave this company, a company that figures out how much things are worth, more than $15 million.

It's ironic, *don't ya think?*

ART.COM

Apparently shipping oddly shaped packages in an industry whose customers need to see the product in person and not in "32-bit hi-color" didn't work.

Employing seventy people, Art.com sold framed prints

of famous paintings and photographs. The company was founded in 1998 as ArtUFrame.com and quickly made its mark in the dot-com dumbass museum when they bought the domain name "Art.com" for an amount in excess of $400,000.

Interestingly, the original owner of the domain name was a helicopter engine manufacturer Advanced Rotary Technologies.

All hell broke loose when the company was sold to Getty Images for $115 million in 1999. Founded by the heir to Getty Oil, Getty Images maintains an archive of over 70,000 images. Originally a business-to-business company, they sell images (and image licenses) to advertising agencies, web shops, product manufacturers, and other companies that need stock photography. Getty Images' main competitor is Corbis, a private company owned by Microsoft's Bill "I can buy and sell your ass" Gates.

Anyway, this was Getty's big go at business-to-consumer. The idea was actually kinda neat-o. See, they have all these images in digital format. Open a website, let people buy posters and crap, and then use all kinds of fancy printing machines to make the print, frame it, and ship it out. That's right, no inventory.

This probably could have been a decent business except for the facts that (a) people still wanna see this stuff in person and (b) the company was built in the dot-com heyday so waaay too much money had already been poured in to ever realize profitability.

Anyway, in May 2001, Getty wised up and dropped Art.com like a hot turd. Later that month, the Art.com domain name and customer list was sold to an online poster retailer, AllWall.com.

CHARITABLEWAY.COM

A dot-com masquerading as a touchy-feely nonprofit company, CharitableWay.com listed hundreds of charities and let people make donations on behalf of other people.

Venture capital firms spent over $43 million on this mess, hoping to find a way to tap into the billions that are donated to charity each year. This was basically the online equivalent of those telemarketing fund-raising companies who skim a nice percentage off the top.

The charities themselves are an afterthought.

Spending $43 million building a website that asks for donations? I couldn't if I tried. Guess they really *were* aspiring to be nonprofit. Har har.

BEAUTYJUNGLE.COM

I'm no makeup expert (not that there's anything wrong with that), but don't you try it on or smudge it at least before you buy it? Far as I know (and apparently what online makeup retailer BeautyJungle.com found out) is that people don't trust the pixels in their computer monitor to compare one shade of red lipstick to another.

And not to play "mister obvious" here, but from the average Joe's perspective, it only takes like two people to sell makeup at the corner store. You sell more makeup, maybe you hire more people. BeautyJungle.com hired around 100 people, sold products at 30% off, and offered free shipping. A great deal for customers, but an automatic fuck for the company.

I'm just pissed cuz I looted through their garbage but couldn't find what they did with all that leftover hand lotion . . . Financed with $23 million and no lotion. Shame.

BeautyJungle.com's charred remains are now owned by FashionMall.com.

IMOTORS.COM

This was a weird one. After $139 million in funding and a seemingly okay business plan (big-ticket items with zero inventory), they still couldn't make it. Seems the big problem here was making a purchase that extravagant without actually testing the product first.

Most people won't buy shoes online—you gotta try on a few pairs before you buy the ones you want (the checkered slip-on Vans, of course). So now we're talking about used cars . . . Apparently you're just supposed to take their word for it that they "inspected" the car and "fixed" all potential problems. Right.

Granted, they let you drive the car post-purchase for ten days and return it for a full refund, "no questions asked." Still, who would risk getting a piece-of-shit car and having to deal with the hassle of taking it back, getting a refund, and going through all the paperwork—when the whole mess could've been avoided if only you had the chance to go for a fifteen-minute test drive . . . ?

iMotors.com's target market: people born yesterday who

were afraid to leave the house, yet still wanted a used car . . . As of this writing, looks like somebody snatched up the iMotors domain name and is trying to do the same thing. Brilliant.

INGREDIENTS.COM

No, you don't get it—the *actual name* of the line of bath and beauty products was Ingredients.com. No, not just the website, but the brand name! Get it? It's so cutting-edge and webby! People will be happy to spend $14 on a small bottle of lotion, just cuz it's so cyberspace-o-rific!

Ugh.

Actually, it's not *completely* dumb. By making your own products and selling them exclusively online, you've fixed two problems: (1) you theoretically pay less for your product, since you're getting it directly from the manufacturer and (2) if people want it, they HAVE to buy it from your site—no competitors are selling it, online or off.

But when the company realized that nobody had heard of them or wanted their shit, they tried selling it at Sephora. Elite by association? I think not.

They shut down their website after $5 million, fifty employees, and about one year of business. Word is they're still trying to sell the stuff on the wholesale market.

Hey I could have given them a real good price on some "lotion." Marketed effectively, it could have generated huge cash flow. My manufacturing costs are nearly nil and my output is predictable and consistent.

Uh-huh.

ZOZA.COM

So fucking weird. There's a shoe store here in Manhattan called something like "Shoes & Belts.com." Their name always weirded me out, not just because you can't have an ampersand in a URL, but because it was so pathetic how EVERYONE thought it was cool to do ANYTHING that even LOOKED Internet-related.

Take Zoza.com. It was a new clothing company started by the two people who started Banana Republic and then sold it to The Gap. Based on that, the VCs who gave them $12 million probably thought they couldn't lose.

They lost.

Getting past the sickening fact that their clothing line was targeted toward dot-commers (did somebody say "blue shirt and khaki pants"?), they operated it *just* like a dot-com. In fact, the original idea was to sell exclusively over the Web, but they realized the same obstacles that every other online clothing retailer did—people like to try stuff on before they buy it.

Here's where they got creative, and I actually give them some credit for having the balls to try—they opened "walk-in websites." This was a network of small stores that, instead of carrying stock, just had samples of every size and color of their merchandise. You'd walk in, try it on, and then order it either from a web terminal in the store or from your computer at home or wherever.

An interesting idea—tiny stores that are cheap and easy to run. On the other hand, from the consumer's standpoint, shoppers experience all of the drawbacks of

e-commerce (paying for shipping . . . waiting . . . needing to be home when the package arrives . . . pain in the
ass to return . . .) with none of the benefits (shopping at
3 A.M. from home, naked, eating warm peanut butter
sandwiches).

MICRO NICHE

PROCESSTREE.COM

Another distributed-computing company, ProcessTree.com went out with a relatively small boom, only blowing around $500,000.

Like PopularPower.com (see p. 31), users would download a little application. The app would periodically download data from ProcessTree, crunch some numbers, and then upload the data back to ProcessTree. A few thousand computers linked up this way, donating their idle CPU time, could rival the processing power of a supercomputer.

This worked kinda like AllAdvantage (see p. 150) in that users not only got "paid" for their involvement, but got a cut from other people they could get to sign up.

The thing is, there's such a small market for this . . . and the people who need that kind of processing power—auto manufacturers, government agencies, laboratories—don't wanna farm out their top-secret problems to 2 million nose-picking AOL users, no matter how well encrypted it is.

Finally, lots o' people just aren't so keen on running other people's processes on *their* 'puter.

They should have kept this in academia, got funded through grants, and cured diseases with it.

SEND.COM

Upscale gift vendor Send.com was another typical example of what could have been a decently profitable niche mail-order business. Instead, they spent around $20 million pretending they were some "bleeding edge" technology company when all they had was a failing business with the clichéd idea of selling average products, available anywhere, over the Internet.

And their products had weirdly pretentious, almost condescending descriptions, such as this gem:

> *An elegant, cream gift box is hand delivered to you revealing nothing about what lies inside. Cradled within its rich interior you see your reward: one, perhaps two bottles of exceptional wine, each hand polished and wrapped in a crisp, white linen napkin.*

I chug wine.

Anyway.

Their business model was basically to get people to pay for sending expensive, overpriced gifts, without the touchy-feely shopping experience. Their audience consisted of lazy rich bastards who didn't really give a shit about the people they were sending gifts to, and who figured the Internet was the easiest way to do it.

Even Send.com's most loyal customers had a use for the site *maybe* once or twice a year. So . . . here you've got a business idea that would appeal to a tiny percentage of the population, who would use it infrequently. Seems somebody didn't do their market research homework . . .

Plus, that wine description was just plain creepy.

BIDLAND.COM

Bidland.com was an application service provider (ASP) with the goal of enabling other websites to run online auctions. They raised and burned through $22 million and employed over seventy people.

This was back in the day when every dot-com thought they needed their own auction. Those were funny days.

Anyway, let me just go on record as saying that there's no fucking way in hell it should ever take that many people to run a fucking ONLINE AUCTION ASP. Maybe if you had a shitload of paying customers and couldn't handle them all . . . but Bidland.com didn't.

If you're a big enough turd that you want to start a business that does exactly what Bidland.com does, and you aren't a programmer, do this: Hire some smart high school kid who knows how to program. Tell him you want to make an auction site that other websites can use. There. Done. That didn't cost $22 million, now did it.

The funny part is that in December 2000, Bidland.com claimed that Telefonica (a real company mind you) promised to enter into a joint venture with them. Dream come true for these dot-commers, right? Anyway, Telefonica soon realized that building something like what Bidland had was easy as pie so they dropped the deal and built their own version, called Katalyx.com.

Bidland.com sued, seeking $500 million in damages. The way I see it, it was like suing a potential customer when you can't sweet talk them enough to finagle them into buying your bullshit. right.

EHOBBIES.COM

eHobbies.com was another e-commerce store that spent millions (specifically, around $20 million) to sell average products, overpriced, available elsewhere for less. They sold radio-controlled cars, modeling glue, shit like that. They also had the requisite articles and chat rooms for hobby geeks.

The site coulda been set up for about $50 a month using a do-it-yourself store like Yahoo!'s, keeping a small warehouse, and hiring employees to handle shipping and fulfillment as they were needed. Grow like a normal business. Or they could have spent millions on the site and hired 150 people they didn't need.

The founders of eHobbies.com opted for the latter, of course.

The deck was stacked against them from the beginning in more ways than they probably knew. First off, the hobby business already had a thriving mail-order component. For hardcore enthusiasts, it wasn't difficult to find retailers with better selections and lower prices. As for beginner hobbyists, the products are so complex and configurable that they require a level of hand-holding and customer support that eHobbies just couldn't provide.

Compounding eHobbies' troubles was the larger issue of the demise of "hobbies" altogether. Kids have been successfully coerced by video games and crappy school curriculums, causing a number of local brick and mortar hobby shops to close. Local hobby shops actually used eHobbies.com to *increase* sales by saying "our prices are cheaper than online."

BUT, that thing I was saying about eHobbies running on a Yahoo! store for cheap? Two of eHobbies' ex-employees bought the site, and, as of this writing, are doing just that. Rad!

Busted!

In August 2000, *The Wall Street Journal* ran a story revealing how a lot of dot-com companies exaggerated the size of their respective markets. Featured in the article was eHobbies.com, who apparently claimed that bird-watching was a $34 billion industry—more than four times as big as movie-going in the United States.

Justifying their estimate, a spokesperson for eHobbies said that the estimate included things like "binoculars, hats, sunglasses, cameras and birdhouses . . . expenses incurred on bird-watching trips, such as gas and hotel bills and the cost of renting a tent . . . sales of log cabins, boats and trucks."

And other stuff eHobbies didn't sell.

OFFICECLICK.COM

OfficeClick.com was a site that targeted administrative professionals (the politically correct way to say "secretaries"), which, it said, was *"one of the most economically powerful and Internet-connected groups of women in the United States."*

Financed with over $35 million, the site offered tips, articles, and help about subjects ranging from scheduling meetings, making travel arrangements, ordering food, and buying office supplies.

The best part is that the site had a "fuck around and surf the Web while you're at work" section called "take a break." The section included horoscopes (why do women's sites *always* have horoscopes?), entertainment news, and a shopping area for buying lotion and shit.

The pitch to advertisers was that one way to get to the boss is to make nice with his or her secretary. But in reality, on the Web, you've just got a site targeting people most marketers try to avoid.

And . . . apparently secretaries don't fuck around on the Web all day and buy lotion.

PLANETRX.COM

Drugs are good. Here in New York City, door-to-door drug delivery is a thriving business.

Or so I've heard.

Funded with about $87.5 million, PlanetRX.com tried to sell prescription and nonprescription drugs, beauty products, and other things that you'd find in your typical corner drugstore. Unfortunately for PlanetRX.com, your "typical corner drugstore" is just where people preferred to buy the stuff.

We can actually learn something from NYC drug dealers here. The lesson being that drug delivery services are good if you are either (a) incapacitated, (b) scared that somebody will see you buying a few tubes of Preparation-H and some condoms, or (c) agoraphobic (a side effect?).

Currently, the average person does not have a need to

buy shampoo over the Internet. This will change as people become lazier, online stores get bigger, and shipping gets faster.

But still.

And now that a lot of local drugstores have started letting you call ahead for prescriptions, there's even more incentive to actually walk or drive down the street to get your drugs your own damn self.

Seems to me the real goldmine here is the middleware, technology and networks that make drugstores talk to other drugstores and to doctors' offices.

Once all the brick-and-mortar drugstores become wired, online drugstores will essentially be nothing but front-end order and delivery services for Rite-Aid.

PARTY LIKE IT'S 1999

URBAN BOX OFFICE

UBO was a collection of entertainment sites targeted toward the "hip-hop" community, which, these days, generally means 14-year-old suburban white kids.

At the end they had a whopping 270 employees and were reportedly burning through more than $3 million per month of their over $35.5 million funding.

"On what?" you ask.

In the mid- to late nineties, "popular hip-hop culture" more often than not meant Rolex watches, Cristal Champagne, Mercedes cars, and all the other "bling bling" portrayed on MTV and the like. I'm not judging, it's just a fact. So that, in combination with excessive dot-com spending in general, translated into insane spending on unnecessary things at UBO . . . for example, they rented Liberty Island—home to the Statue of Liberty—for their launch party.

Yes, the whole island.

Incidentally, I heard it was a kick-ass party. No, I wasn't invited, which sucks cuz they were famous for the "quality" of their female employees . . . hey that's just what I heard . . .

Anyway.

After doing business for less than a year, the company filed for bankruptcy and disappeared.

CARCLUB.COM

CarClub.com was essentially a middleman—they referred car buyers to car sellers, taking a piece of the action. Additionally, they acted like a ghetto version of AAA, where members paid $5.99 per month to receive discounts on gasoline and insurance, but not towing.

Witness the poster child for reckless dot-com spending. They hired people to promote the company by passing out $5 bills at gas stations and freeway off-ramps. They gave away $15 Amazon.com gift certificates to people who signed up for their free services, not realizing (or more likely not caring) that the same person could sign up 500 times with 500 Hotmail accounts and buy the whole friggin store . . .

CarClub members received a CarClub MasterCard that entitled members to a 10% discount when used for up to $200 worth of gas each month. But the card worked wherever MasterCard was accepted, not just designated gas stations . . . so . . . for $72 per year in dues, users basically received $240 per year in cash to spend anywhere . . .

And in the end, the whole thing was a useless concept that added surprisingly little value to the whole process. Some people thought that using the site would help them avoid dealing with annoying car salespeople. Not true— you go through the site, answer twenty-five questions, give all sorts of information, and after a ten-minute online interview, all they really did was forward your info to some local dealership. You still had to deal with all the car dealer BS. For this they skimmed a few bucks off every deal . . . not to mention that Ford dumped $40 million into this cesspool, likely counting on all those referrals . . .

200 employees later, they went out of business.

As of this writing, it looks as if somebody snatched up their domain name and launched a new site . . .

ETOYS.COM

There's surprisingly little that needs to be said about online toy retailer eToys.com. It was one of the best-known e-commerce companies in the world and was a huge operation—they employed over 1,000 people and managed to flush $200 million down the toilet before they went out of business.

What it basically comes down to is that you have to have a compelling reason to draw shoppers to your store, especially if you need to profit $200 million on TOYS just to break even.

Toys aren't generally impulse items. Most people still prefer to buy them locally, avoiding shipping charges and saving delivery time. During the crucial 2000 holiday season, eToys.com only did about *half* the business they had predicted.

This could have been a nice, small, profitable business. It could have grown organically. It could have made a few people a good amount of money, and who knows, could have eventually taken over the toy-selling world.

At one point, eToys.com was "worth" over $1 billion. And that's all I have to say about that.

Established toy retailer Kay-Bee Toy Stores ended up buying the domain name and lauched a new eToys.com in late 2001.

COLLEGEHIRE.COM

A spin-off of software maker Trilogy, CollegeHire.com was a job board with a twist—they exclusively targeted soon-to-graduate college students.

They traveled around to different college campuses and held group interviews. The thing is, interviews weren't for any specific company. Rather, CollegeHire.com would interview and test students, and then pitch them to employers.

"Congratulations! You've received an offer from [insert fucked company here]."

To be fair, CollegeHire.com recruited for traditional businesses also, but at the time, traditional companies were competing with dot-coms willing to hire English majors with no experience, call them "web architects," and pay them $100,000 a year.

"As the number of technology jobs continues to far outpace the number of technology graduates, the industry's most respected companies such as Amazon are looking for every edge to reach students," CollegeHire.com told News .com when asked about their alliance with Amazon.

A sign of the times, not only were employers bribing new hires with huge signing bonuses and other perks, but so were *recruiters*. CollegeHire.com held raffles when they visited different colleges, giving away PDAs, Sega Dreamcasts, Cancún vacations, and a few BMWs.

The company ceased operations on June 1, 2001.

MARCHFIRST

The result of a ground-breaking merger between traditional consultancy Whittman-Hart and web shop USWeb/CKS, MarchFirst was a poster child of fucked web consultancies.

Let's back up a bit.

This book is made possible by investors and by marketing people at mega web shops like MarchFirst.

USWeb/CKS BUILT WEBSITES. Yeah they were a "next generation B2B solution using best-of-breed e-tools blah blah blah bullshit bullshit bullshit," but really, they built fucking websites. Perhaps good websites, but websites nonetheless. Their purpose was twofold: (1) to build websites and (2) to hype up the industry, building demand.

I was one such web monkey. See the introduction to this book for more info on that . . .

Anyway, building websites is relatively easy. That's not to say that *everyone* can do it, nor that anyone would be *interested* in learning how. And like playing bass guitar, it's possible to suck and be a rock star, or play like Flea and be homeless. Still, generally, it's not brain surgery (which I'm assuming is kinda tricky).

Rocket science I don't think is so hard.

Regardless, I'm an idiot and even *I* was able to build a successful small business building websites. Thing is, we didn't charge millions to build a five-minute CGI email form. That's why we're still around.

See, in the late nineties, practically every high school kid in America started building websites. The big web shops realized that they wouldn't be able to compete, they wouldn't be able to keep the charade going forever—the charade that the work they were doing was ingenious. They started promising all kinds of things, making up new words, "new economy bullshit speak."

Not only did web shops like USWeb/CKS convert a lot of suckers into paying customers, but they fooled the media, which in turn fooled the general public. At that point, every Tom, Dick, and Harry started spending millions building stupid-ass websites that they believed could CHANGE THE WORLD (see *this whole fucking book*).

My point: Anyone can build a website. Not just anyone can be a skilled management consultant.

Whittman-Hart fucked up when they merged with this puppy. It was only a matter of time before the web division couldn't scam as many people and started crumbling while small, boutique web shops flourished. That said, there's always gonna be a need for companies that can build quality websites, just like there's always gonna be a need for auto mechanics. But that's just it—next time your mechanic charges you $500,000 to replace your flux capacitor, open your fuckin' eyes.

At one point worth about $14 billion (yes, with a "b"), the bankrupt MarchFirst sold most of their assets to Divine, a VC turned software company, for around $60 million.

Those Were the Days . . .

In June 2000, MarchFirst launched a $50 million advertising campaign. They said the campaign's goal wasn't to land new biz—it was to help recruit new employees.

In total, MarchFirst has laid off more than 2,100 people.

GIVE IT AWAY NOW

ECIRCLES.COM

eCircles.com was an online photo album. Users could go to the site, register, and upload photos and other files and messages with the intention of sharing them with friends and family in their "eCircle."

Despite raising $24 million in venture capital, eCircles' service was 100% free to use. Here's the brilliant revenue model: They set up a system where friends and family members in the same "eCircle" could recommend products to one another from participating e-commerce stores. eCircles was hoping to make a commission on the deal.

I dunno, the first time a friend or family member of mine spams me with "perfect gift-giving ideas!" from Amazon or wherever, he or she'll have some 'splaining to do . . .

I really don't see how anyone could have ever thought there was a real business in there, screaming to get out . . . I mean sure, AOL has forums 'n' shit—but they sell dialups. Blah.

eCircles.com's assets were acquired by alumni information service Classmates.com, who has, far as I can tell, a clever revenue model—charge people to get in touch with out-of-contact friends.

THEGLOBE.COM

Well here's where it all began.

TheGlobe.com was one of the first pure-BS dot-coms to go public, resulting in two multizillionaire twenty-three-year-old white guys who told CNBC they were going to "change the world" and build a multibillion-dollar business by selling ads on their BBS.

Really nothing more than an electronic bulletin board system, TheGlobe offered message boards and homepages and all the stuff people were paying $20 a month to AOL for . . . hence TheGlobe's popularity (read: it was free).

In November 1998, they were really the first dot-com to get a multibillion-dollar market cap despite not making or doing anything that generated revenue. Opening day, their stock shot up from $9 to $97 per share. At the time, it was the largest first-day gain of any IPO in history.

TheGlobe's IPO started the feeding frenzy that was the fodder for this book (and TheGlobe.com's co-founder Stephan Paternot's book). So for that, TheGlobe.com, rest assured that your efforts weren't a *complete* waste of time and money . . .

EVOICE.COM

eVoice.com spent over $51,000,000 (looks good with all the zeros) developing their online, business-to-consumer voice mail company. Yeah yeah we all know that answering machines cost $20 and you can already get inexpensive voice mail service from your local phone company, but still, it's WEBBY!

eVoice did have some cool features, namely that it would automatically email users digital audio files of their messages, which was handy if you used eVoice for home and wanted to get your messages from work. Then again, what answering machine or voice mail service *doesn't* let you check your messages remotely. None. They all do.

Their main advantage? When they first started signing people up, their service was free—then they thought they could get away with the old switch-a-roo (which I whole-heartedly support, by the way). Knowing that people hate dealing with phone companies, eVoice probably figured that their users were too fat and lazy to deal with the phone company in getting their service disconnected from eVoice.

Apparently eVoice was wrong—they started charging and thus their customers started dropping like flies.

$51 million and about 100 employees were pushed into this hole by investors, including Idealab and Nokia. The site shut down in June 2001, but word is their assets have been purchased by an undisclosed party . . . time will tell.

BITLOCKER.COM

This was actually sort of a cool technology. BitLocker.com had an easy-to-use system for building dynamic websites that required no database or application platforms on the server. It competed mainly with rapid application development (RAD) environments like Microsoft's Active Server Pages, Allaire's ColdFusion, and PHP.

The RAD environments also required databases such as Microsoft's SQL Server, MySQL, Oracle, etc.

So basically, it was useful, it was easy—oh yeah, and it was FREE. Need I say more?

They prided themselves on helping their "customers" (if Frito-Lay sent me chips for free, would I be their "customer"?) save money because they no longer had to spend "thousands of dollars" on application platforms, databases, and staff.

I can see it now, "At Pud's Auto Emporium, we save you THOUSANDS of dollars by giving you cars for FREE, NO STRINGS ATTACHED!"

Awesome! Can I get some funding?

\<hitting myself on the head>

Originally funded with $10 million and employing forty people, BitLocker closed on June 15, 2001. In August 2001, their technology was bought by a company called "Bungo."

Fitting.

SIXDEGREES.COM

All I could say about SixDegrees.com when they closed down was "Thank God"—I think I received more email spam from this company than from anywhere else.

The company's deal was simple—if everyone is connected to everyone else by at most six degrees of separation, and everyone signed up on the site, anyone could contact anyone else via networking through their six degrees. A cool idea, and one that's perfect for the Internet. They could have even charged money for contact information and prolly woulda made a bundle.

Thing is, the idea is simple enough that pretty much any programmer could have developed it. There was no need for YouthStream Media to acquire the company for $125 million, as they did in January 2000, just to shut it down eleven months later.

SixDegrees.com was also a study in dot-com PR hype—they claimed to have 3 million members, when really, a "member" was just an email address. Users of the site sign in all their friends, who sometimes signed up (after being bombarded with spam), never to return to the site again—yet they were counted amongst the regular users.

Righteous.

ZELERATE

Okay, finally something I know a little about . . . cuz ya know . . . so far in this book I've basically been making shit up ya know . . .

Zelerate.com was yet another fiasco funded by Idealab (I really should have just let *them* write this book). Zelerate.com had only one flaw. Allow me to explain . . .

They created an e-commerce platform, which is basically a piece of software that performs tasks like online catalog maintenance, shopping cart, check out, and other e-commerce functions. If you had a business that wanted to sell stuff online, using Zelerate's software was a viable option.

So far, that's exactly what my business, PK Interactive, did. I developed a piece of software that did essentially the same thing as Zelerate's. My small business was reasonably successful, eventually grew to five employees, and was nicely profitable doing just that.

But Zelerate went out of business.

Wanna hear my secret?

WE CHARGED PEOPLE ACTUAL MONEY FOR OUR PRODUCT. That's right, people would send us money, and in exchange we'd send them a copy of our software. We also made money by charging customers for extended support and maintenance. Brilliant, I know . . .

Zelerate missed that one point, the part about *selling* their software. The idea behind Zelerate was that their software was open-source, which means that it was *free*. They only planned to make money on maintenance and support.

One reason why maintenance and support didn't build a business was cuz the target audience for their software was web developers—web shops or in-house developers. Companies don't pay their developers to sit around and do nothing—they pay them to support and maintain their sites.

And . . . rumor was that the software was originally developed for eToys.com (see p. 125), another Idealab-funded turd. Even though the software was seen as somewhat of a nightmare, they tried to make a buck off it, since they certainly weren't selling many toys . . .

Kind of like giving away free dog shit then asking people to pay you to tell them how to rub it in their nostrils.

One good thing about the software being free and open-source is that even though Zelerate basically no longer exists, their software is still being developed, used, and maintained by the open-source community.

Funded with $10 million, their demise kinda makes you realize how unnecessary the prolonged existence of this company was in the first place . . .

FREEWORKS.COM

FreeWorks.com was an ASP for businesses that provided the ability to populate and process forms for payroll and other accounting information.

As their name suggests, they didn't charge any money for their services.

Duh.

But it's deeper than that.

This was another company wrapped up in what I call the "spin-off" scam. It's when a company makes a product that would be the logical next step for some other, established company. For example, an online accounting system was a logical next step for companies like Quicken and QuickBooks, who make accounting software that you have to run on your own computer.

Get millions in funding and beat them to the punch. Then grow the popularity of the product—get people hooked on it—by giving it away for free.

When the time comes for QuickBooks, for example, to develop their online accounting system, the hope is that they'd find it too cumbersome and expensive to compete with the new company's product, so they'd just snatch up the new company's and call it their own—or they'd call it a spin-off.

Problem is, if nobody buys the new company, they've only got so much money to burn before they're screwed and the established company squashes them with a more ubiquitous product.

And the rest . . . is history.

B2C2B2MCD'S

ZING.COM

Zing.com was basically nothing more than a $14 million FTP site. Another remote storage site (see *MySpace.com*). In other words, a place where people can log in and dump their files. Like the others, Zing.com was cool with garnering 1.7 million eyeballs (actually, 3.4 million actual *eyeballs* I guess) rather than generating actual revenue.

But . . . their first business was even more hilarious. Zing.com was originally known as Streamix, a company that made—get this—a piece of software you could DOWNLOAD so that you could LOOK AT ADVERTISEMENTS WHILE YOU WERE WAITING FOR PAGES TO LOAD.

HAhAH AH Hah ahahAH HAahahaha HAHAhahah hahaah haah HA Hahah aha hHAAHAHa hahahahah haha HAha HAHAHah AHA Hah ahahah aHA HAHAhaha HAHAh ah aha Hah hahahaha HA Hahaha hah Ah AHahaAHhaah ahHah aah HAHa haH AHHAHAha ahahah ahah AHHAAHAHAHAHAHAHA Hah aha hAH ahahahah AH haah ahahahahahah HA HAHAahah HAH HA HA HA Haha HAha haah aHAHHAAH hah aha hAHAH HA hah haHAAH ah HAh.

Oh my sides.

HAhahaAH ahahH Ahah aha haha ha ha.

Okay.

Anyway, getting back to their second success at failure, Zing.com. When they realized that eyeballs weren't gonna pay the bills (unless you're in the famed Colombian black market organ trade), they started to sell merchandise with your pictures on them. Mugs and T-shirts and shit with a picture of your dog or whatever. Huge money maker, as you could surely imagine.

Zing differentiated themselves from the many other on-line photo storage services (Shutterfly.com, Ofoto.com, etc.) in that Zing.com was (supposedly) working with hardware manufacturers to integrate the website with their devices. In other words, you plug your Nikon digital camera into your computer, push the "Zing" button, and the camera software automatically loads your pictures onto Zing's website.

So like, why is there even a need for this service? Filled up your hard drive? No you didn't. Don't know how to email a picture to your friends? Yes you do.

Well apparently Zing couldn't figure it out either—they shut down their website in June 2001, and as of this writing they are apparently "refocusing" their efforts on becoming an "infrastructure provider."

GREATENTERTAINING.COM

GreatEntertaining.com gave party planning advice and sold related merchandise. Their original target market was the general public, kids' birthday parties, and such. In other words, they had $35 million private funding TO SELL FUCKING PARTY FAVORS ON THE NET.

Problem was no parent would order Barney and Tele-tubby shit from them and risk late delivery, leading to little Johnny and his friends eating out of dog food bowls and blowing up condom balloons.

Which brings me to my next lesson.

You can generally predict that a dot-com company is

about to join the prestigious *Fuckedcompany Hall-of-Fame* when they switch their business model from business-to-consumer (B2C) to business-to-business (B2B).

The idea behind this classic move is simple—when you're selling to businesses rather than to consumers, you have fewer customers and fewer marketing channels to deal with. This, of course, enables you to cut out salespeople, marketing people, customer service people, and other people in place to support a larger customer base.

Incidentally, a lot of companies that made the B2C/B2B switch didn't actually *have* a larger customer base to speak of, but they had people *in place* to support one . . . and that's the important part, right? Right.

Anyway, I was saying . . .

When GreatEntertaining realized shit was about to hit the fan, they made the switch to B2B. Their new targets were corporations and professional party planners. Along with the switch to B2B went forty of their sixty employees.

A few months later they went out of business.

And the party was officially moved back into my pants.

MULTITUDE.COM

Multitude.com was an online video game company founded in 1996 by a video game industry veteran. They made an online game called FireTeam that required players to wear headsets for voice communication during the game.

Apparently the game sucked and pretty much nobody played it, but the voice-over-IP (VoIP) technology was kinda all right.

Or at least they pretended it was.

Voilà—a few years later they ditched the game biz and tried to market their VoIP thing. $45 million later, the move kinda looked like a last-ditch effort to make the company look like something somebody might wanna buy . . . but no luck.

Essentially, they moved into an industry that already had competitors with better products—who were giving them away for free (see *LipStream.com*).

BID.COM

As of this writing, Bid.com is still in business. I'm listing them here, however, because they're basically a different company now. At one point, they were Canada's largest on-line auction site (eBay for hosers?). They grew pretty big, started trading on Nasdaq, and eventually realized they couldn't make any money (unlike eBay), and gave up.

They even posted the ever-clichéd "good-bye, sorry it had to end this way"–type message on their site.

Then I turn around and suddenly they're back, but this time they're selling auction software to OTHER BUSI-NESSES. Would you throw a wad of money at a software company who failed USING THEIR OWN SOFTWARE? "Shit, *we* couldn't make it work, but maybe *you* can!"

I'm a Little Teapot

The best thing that ever happened to Bid.com was a fake press release that was posted on a Yahoo! message board. The press release discussed an $89 million alliance between Bid.com and AOL. Immediately following the posting of the fake release, Bid.com's volume jumped from just over 150,000 shares per hour to over 1 million shares, and the price jumped over 5%. The perpetrator, a twenty-five-year-old wholesale tool dealer, got away scot-free, explaining that he was "just letting some steam out."

$100 SHOPPING SPREE IF YOU READ THIS CHAPTER!

STICKY NETWORKS

This product sucked ass. It's amazing what people were able to bilk other people out of their money for. I guess it's the old "If we get 0.1% of 1% we'll all be rich" line.

Gets 'em every time.

Sticky Networks was a company that made a stupid, stupid thing called "Stickies" (see *Third Voice*). A sticky was a little doohickey that developers could put into their websites. The purpose of it was to display little context-specific pop-up menus when a user rolled his or her mouse over an image.

It was a cute little Java applet (yeah . . . ugh) bell-n-whistle that some kid definitely would have put on her Geocities site in maybe 1995, but there's no way any serious e-commerce site (their target) would go near such a toy.

Nobody got it, nobody used it. There are a billion equally simple little Java applets out there, but I can't think of any that took THIRTY EMPLOYEES and $15 MILLION IN BACKING. HOLY SHIT—yes it's true. How they thought they would make any of that money back, I've no clue.

The funniest part is that the company thought they could swindle $5,000 per month per license for the thing. Anyone who knows Flash or Java could program their own version of a "Sticky" without using the "Sticky Networks" technology. But why would they even want to?

The company lasted a mere seven months.

In an interview with *Red Herring* discussing Sticky's demise, Sticky Networks' founder said that "the market wasn't ready for the company's offerings."

Apparently he still doesn't get it.

SAVE.COM

Who the fuck did they think would go online and print out a coupon just to save 25 cents on a bottle of apple juice?

Save.com was just that—yet another site trying to make billions from coupons (see *Meals.com, ShoppingList.com, Dash.com*). Seemed most of their coupons were either so small that they weren't worth the hassle, or worse yet, were just advertisements.

Yeah yeah we all know that a coupon is really just an ad, but I'm talking about "coupons" for a "free catalog" from an electronics store, or even a "coupon" to "save big on clearance merchandise!" on an e-commerce site where the sale was readily available without said "coupon." Most retailers and manufacturers didn't want to deal with Save.com, partially cuz they'd never heard of 'em, but also because Save.com required users to install a browser plug-in to properly print coupons with bar codes on them—no guarantee that they'd print correctly.

Generally, it was low-income families who used 25-cents-off coupons—not the most web savvy audience in the world. A nice thought, but far from lucrative. Majority investor Valassis took an estimated $5 million (or so) hit.

CYBERGOLD.COM

Spammers, parasitic crapweasels who send mass amounts of unsolicited email, are the lowest form of scum on the Internet (cybersquatters are a close second). Nevertheless, verified, working email addresses are worth a mint. Email address collection is big business.

Enter CyberGold.com.

CyberGold.com was a bullshit company that referred users to affiliate websites where they were to sign up for newsletters, fill out questionnaires (see *FreeRide.com*), request price quotes, stuff like that. In return, users received "cash" (spare change) from CyberGold—and TRUCKLOADS OF SPAM from all the shit they'd signed up for.

The company filed to go public in May 1999, when IPO was the name of the game, and, somehow, investors were buying. The $45 million IPO happened in September 1999.

The company was losing millions, but the worst part was that they actually had competitors. Many of them. In April 2000, CyberGold's chief competitor, MyPoints.com, bought CyberGold for $157 million in stock.

In July 2001, United Airlines' venture capital subsidiary bought MyPoints.com/CyberGold for around $112 million—and quickly flushed CyberGold down the cyber-toilet.

DASH.COM

Okay here's how it worked. You'd go to Dash.com, sign up, and download *DashBar*, their 100K browser plug-in. With the plug-in installed, a little window appeared at the bottom of your browser that informed you of discounts and coupons available at the shopping site you happened to be visiting at that moment.

With $50 million in venture capital and 100 people on staff, they thought that shopping sites would pay them to be included in the DashBar system. You know, kinda like those ValuePak coupon books you get in the mail—the advertiser gets new business and the ValuePak snail-mail spammer people get a kickback. Except . . . rather than get the discount at checkout, most specials worked more like a rebate, where Dash.com would actually mail a check to the user after the sale was complete.

Well that's odd. Why'd they do it that way? Why didn't they just get partner sites to discount users as they checked out?

Neat as DashBar would have been, Dash's problem was that most of their clients were either (a) out of business, (b) out of money, or (c) drastically lowering their marketing budgets. So . . . word is that the Dash.com people just signed up for affiliate programs on various websites where they'd get a cut of sales that they referred. Anyone can sign up for affiliate programs. Your grandma can make a free Geocities page and be an "authorized Amazon.com affiliate," referring sales to Amazon.com and getting a cut.

Anyway, word is that Dash.com signed up for all these affiliate programs and then pretended that those sites were offering rebates—when in actuality, Dash.com was just passing their affiliate commission back to the user.

Great deal for the user, sucked for Dash. Dash.com terminated their service in June 2001, and as of this writing are apparently still sseeaarrcchhiinngg for a buyer.

EPOD.COM

With $18 million in funding, most notably from Macromedia, ePod.com sought to change the world of online marketing—specifically, the evil banner ad. Their idea was to make banner ads with their own e-commerce backend.

For example, let's say you were on RollingStone.com,

One and the Same

Don't confuse ePod.com with ePods. Although both are featured in this book, they are different, unrelated companies.

In December 2000, ePods went out of business. ePod.com then issued a statement urging folks not to confuse the two, and that ePod.com was "still thriving."

Two months later, ePod.com went out of business too.

reading about a band you like. A banner ad for CDNow.com, one of ePod's affiliates, would appear. Rather than clicking on the banner ad and being transported to CDNow.com's website, you could do all your shopping on the little banner ad without ever having to leave RollingStone.com.

The idea makes sense, but unfortunately, there were two key ingredients here that wouldn't last.

Firstly, the ad market. It bottomed out and that was that, people stopped buying ads—many companies that used to buy ads were simply out of business. Paradoxically, often cuz of their huge ad budgets . . .

Secondly, profits. In the days before e-commerce companies cared about making a profit, ePod.com was golden. Companies would run ePod ads promoting great deals on sale items. Problem was that not only were margins razor thin, if they were profitable at all, but then the vendor had to give a cut to ePod, thus sucking away any profit they might have made.

ALLADVANTAGE.COM

"Pay-to-Surf" was a big money-burning inferno in the late nineties. Here's how this one worked: Users used AllAdvantage's special web browser, which showed ads as they surfed—and as a special side bonus, collected their personal information. AllAdvantage.com would then give cash to users in exchange for viewing these ads.

There was just SO much fucking money being thrown into online advertising that this scam may have worked for a few weeks, even months. As soon as advertisers saw what was going on though . . . it was pretty much over.

An analyst with Jupiter Media Metrix summed it up when he told News.com, "Magazines don't pay people to read a magazine."

Furthermore, it was basically a multilevel marketing thing (Amway anyone?) in that users got a cut from *other* users who they could get to sign up. This fast became an Internet plague, with AllAdvantage douchemonkeys spamming all over the place trying to get other dumbasses to sign up.

The company had received over $131 million in financing. According to a filing in early June 2000, AllAdvantage paid $32.7 million to members from December 1999 to March 2000—but generated only $9.1 million revenue for the same period.

Brilliant.

CHAPTER FOURTEEN

PORTALS TO NOWHERE

GO.COM

This was Disney's portal that was designed to basically compete with Yahoo!.

Okay, before we begin I'm gonna clarify, once and for all, the difference between a "portal" and a "search engine." If you already know the difference, skip the next two paragraphs and send me $10.

Search engines are essentially huge databases that scour the Internet to collect all the data they can find. They have little programs called "spiders" that constantly crawl around the Web (get it?) and feed the search engine's database. As a user, you can search the database and hope to find whatever (porn) it is you're looking for. Example: Google.com.

Portals kinda work the same as search engines from the user's standpoint—you type in a keyword and it gives you matching results. The difference is that a portal's database is generally populated by human beings, rather than by automatic spiders. Portals don't contain as much data, but they are often better organized and the data is usually more relevant to your search. Example: Yahoo!.

Oh yeah, Disney. So . . . long story short, Disney figured out that their unpopular portal was a waste of time and money, so they trashed it—taking an over $815 million write-off.

Disney later revived the Go.com domain and put up a site that basically contains news feeds from Disney properties ABC and ESPN, and a list of links to other Disney sites.

Friends with the Enemy

In February 1999, search engine company GoTo.com sued Disney, claiming that Disney's Go.com logo was too similar to GoTo.com's logo, and was causing confusion.

The case reportedly settled with Disney paying GoTo.com more than $20 million.

Ironically, GoTo.com now provides the core search services on the new Go.com site.

QUEPASA.COM

Yay, a "portal and community" site for Spanish speakers. Before selling their remaining assets for pennies, they had free email, news feeds, even chat rooms! People, regular people, actually bought public shares of this company in a $68 million IPO. Ugh.

To start one of these, you need $15 and a free Geocities website. That's how Fuckedcompany.com started, that's pretty much how all the big community sites started.

In November 2000, Gary Trujillo, chairman of this fiasco, sold 115,000 shares at 25 cents a piece. At one point this stock was up over 15 bucks. He thought he was gonna be muy rico.

I'm gonna go watch Telemundo now. Buenas noches.

SCAPE.COM

Scape.com was an Australian entertainment portal targeted toward sixteen- to thirty-nine-year-olds. The company attempted to make money from advertising, as well as from collecting and selling user profile information.

Scape.com started with $44 million and made all the classic mistakes.

Huge advertising expenses . . . Billboards, radio, TV, you name it.

Even though they had over 100 employees, they hired web consultancy Razorfish to develop their site. Consultancies are good if you're not primarily in the Internet business. If you're a law firm, retail store, manufacturer . . . they're fine.

BUT IF YOU'RE A FUCKING WEBSITE, BUILD IT YOUR OWN GODDAM SELF. Besides saving a shitload of money, you'll have people around who actually know how the damn thing works.

Also, their website was so "hip," so "edgy," that it was annoying to use. Flash, Java, pop-up windows, gray-on-white text . . . That sort of shit will so become a thing of the past.

HEADLIGHT.COM

Distance learning is one of the few truly perfect applications for the Internet. Unfortunately for HeadLight.com, spending $10 million to build a site that brokers *other companies'* e-learning products was not the way toward fame and fortune.

HeadLight.com started out as basically an e-learning portal, sending people off to other sites and services, hoping to take a cut of the action.

They soon realized how lame that was and developed a proprietary delivery system for different types of distance learning courseware. Perhaps useful, but certainly not worth $10 million.

And really, computer-based training (CBT) sucks. On-line versions of user manuals . . . although one of my first clients when I first started consulting was the National Guard—I scored some CBT for driving tanks and blowing up grenades 'n shit. That kinda rocked.

I got it—3D, virtual-reality shoot-'em-up "Learning Microsoft Excel" courseware. Rad.

CHAPTER
FIFTEEN

IF IT AIN'T
BROKE,
FIX IT

FINANCIALPRINTER.COM

Hoping to cash in on 1999's IPO frenzy, FinancialPrinter .com opened their doors with the help of a reported $19 million in funding. The purpose of FinancialPrinters.com was to help public and soon-to-be-public companies create and distribute legal and other documents. Specifically the company would print and ship registration statements, prospectuses (yes that's the plural for "prospectus," eat me very much), and the like.

And for the *truly* fucked companies, FinancialPrinter.com even had a sort of do-it-yourself-IPO-registration-writer-thingy-majigy where executive assclowns could plug in the name of their company and other pertinent info and insert it into a generic registration statement.

Anyone remember *Mad Libs*?

Besides the tumbling market and delayed IPOs that rendered this company virtually useless, they just couldn't compete in the market. Financial printing is one of the most time-sensitive and exacting areas of the printing biz, and few people were willing to risk their career and their company's future by sending files off to some faceless website with a questionable future . . .

In an obvious attempt to quell fears of their inevitable demise, here was one of the "Frequently Asked Questions" from their website:

Q: Is your company financially stable?

A: Yes, FinancialPrinter.com is a business unit of Conscium Inc., a well capitalized private company. Conscium's in-

vestors include top-tier venture firms, as well as several strategic law firm and corporate partners.

Yeah that and a dollar'll get you a bucketful of kiss-my-ass.

FinancialPrinter.com effectively ceased all operations on Friday, January 26, 2001.

ELAW.COM

Lawyers are notorious for generally being some of the most computer-illiterate people on the planet. With the possible exception of being able to rock a query like nobody's business on LexisNexis, most of 'em still use WordPerfect.

Regardless, maybe LexisNexis gave hope to eLaw.com, which was basically a big library of briefs, memos, and other legal documents from participating, allied law firms and attorneys.

Besides the fact that eLaw.com couldn't get lawyers to use the Internet (something that will change, but didn't happen soon enough) and that it was difficult to change in two years the way lawyers have been doing business for a hundred years, there were privacy concerns. It was tough getting attorneys to upload sensitive documents to the site.

Law is basically recession-proof. In fact during this whole dot-com implosion, there was an explosion in the number of work-related and shareholder lawsuits. Shit, they could have stayed in business just dealing with all the "cease and desist" letters I've received in the past couple of years running Fuckedcompany.com . . .

Still, they ended just like any other dot-com, blaming the economy rather than just writing it off as an idea that, at the time, didn't work. Anyway, I probably would have blamed lawyers . . . just cuz everyone does . . . ya know?

eLaw.com blew through $12.5 million and laid off around forty-four people. Silver lining: Some of them were probably lawyers.

FOODLINE.COM

When the Web first started gaining mainstream acceptance, one of the first things everyone thought of were online restaurant reservation systems (and gift registries). Seemed simple enough—I could put my own name in the reservation book rather than calling somebody and having them do it for me.

Making it happen involved two parts: (1) building the website and (2) the part nobody mentioned, building the software for the restaurants, installing the computers, hooking them up with high-speed Internet access, dealing with mission-critical customer service (restaurant to Foodline: "We can't access tonight's reservations!"), and so on.

Besides the obstacles mentioned above, a few other problems existed. First, nobody trusted online reservations to actually be there when they arrived at the restaurant. Second, turning on your computer, going to the website, registering, and filling out the appropriate forms were generally more of a hassle than just picking up the phone and dialing.

Foodline.com had around 150 employees and spent about $13 million on this bomb.

It was a neat solution, but the problem wasn't BIG enough to justify the existence of this company.

Foodline.com is trying to give it another go, servicing just Boston and New York.

METALSPECTRUM.COM

There will be Harvard Business School cases looking at all of these single-material broker sites like MetalSpectrum.com and MetalSite.com, and it'll be the first time the words "crack addled" will be used in a HBS case study.

MetalSpectrum, whose slogan was "We define the metals marketplace" (ha ha) opened shop as a business-to-business marketplace for buying and selling specialty metals such as aluminum, stainless steel, and brass.

In the height of dot-com cockiness, they basically declared victory over competing metal marketplaces that had been around since the 1800s. Trading raw materials is undoubtedly more efficient when executed online (you don't have to "try it on" first), but did they really think everyone would just instantly give up how they'd been doing business for the last 100 years and go to the Web?

If getting companies to accept online marketplaces could work at all (which it most likely will, of course), it's gonna take time and patience—two things that Internet companies aren't famous for.

MetalSpectrum burned $40 million and about eighty employees in LESS than twelve months and shut down. Competitor MetalSite.com burned through about $35 million.

These turkeys were gone from the git-go.

COMRO.COM

Commercial Realty Online (Comro.com) attempted to "provide a better way for owners and agents of commercial properties to market their space for lease."

Another real-estate listing service?

Basically.

This was yet another specialized site run by people with little experience in their industry. I'm no real-estate expert (far from it—I'm being ripped off in NYC), but I know that real-estate brokers are some of the most annoying, difficult people to work with. I know that existing real-estate listing services have to bug the hell out of brokers to get the info on available space.

Brokers don't do what they're told—which led to the downfall of this site.

On a side note, Comro.com was another winner selected as a "Forbes Best of the Web" (a.k.a. the "Short These Stocks" list).

HOMEBYTES.COM

HomeBytes.com was an online real-estate brokerage. They were actually the first website licensed as a real-estate broker in all fifty states. They helped people buy and sell homes, charging sellers a $599 flat fee for listing and a 3% commission on closing.

They'd received over $25 million in venture capital, some of it coming from AOL and some of it coming from LandAmerica Financial Group, one of the country's largest providers of real-estate services. Bring in traffic from AOL, have LandAmerica close the deal, perfect!

Except nobody gave a shit.

The companies used neat-o technology to produce 360-degree "walk-around" views of interiors and exteriors. It was supposed to "revolutionize the industry!"

But it didn't.

They bought Owners.com. Founded in 1995, it was the first real-estate company on the Web. Sellers paid a small flat rate, no broker commissions.

Still nobody gave a shit.

Why not?

Online real-estate brokers are competing not only with other online real-estate brokers (including eHome.com, eRealty.com, and zipRealty.com), but also with traditional agents. Traditional agents promote themselves individually, as their own brands. They place ads, they call, they can help you figure out what you should buy by learning about your job, your interests, your family, your lifestyle.

Conversely, online brokerage companies market themselves by sending out automated emails based on checkboxes that were filled out on their site. Most people needed more hand-holding, especially inexperienced buyers. Furthermore, HomeBytes.com was perceived as a faceless out-of-town entity and was not trusted by enough sellers.

Anyway, would you buy a house based on a picture you saw on the Web? Emailing a real-estate agent in another state?

"Uhh, so how's the kitchen."

"Oh, it's very nice."

"You say how many bedrooms?"

"[Including the mattress over the garage and the shed out back?] Six."

Fuck that.

ZOHO.COM

Zoho.com was a hyped-up "e-procurement" business, where hotels could team up and buy products in bulk. You know, like those little shampoos. Ice buckets. Probably those toilet paper ribbon things that say "sanitized for your protection."

Basically, 'twas a specialized, business-to-business version of Mercata.com (see p. 37).

One of the hurdles faced by these companies is that they charged a transaction fee or percentage of the sale to the SELLERS. Not only that, but it likely wouldn't integrate into the seller's existing ERP system.

Zoho: "Print" the order, fill it out, ship it, and then enter the order number back into the Zoho system.

Seller: How much extra work is that? Print the order? Fuck you.

To make matters worse, they had a lot of competition. Often that's not such a big deal, but think about it: The only way a business like this could truly work is if they have critical mass. The idea is to group up hotel buyers and get bulk discounts on stuff, but with so many competitors (and some hotel chains doing it in-house), it was impossible.

Their investors included Starwood Hotels (owner of Sheraton and W brands), Harrah's of Las Vegas, and Dell. The company estimated a potential market of $150 billion worldwide. Despite all this hooha, they managed to blow through around $50 million and over 200 employees in about a year and a half.

I'VE NO FUCKING CLUE

DIGISCENTS

I'd make Fuckedcompany.com smell like peas.

That was the thinking behind Digiscents' flagship product, iSmell. iSmell was a peripheral you could plug into your computer that would make websites and other computer programs *smell*. The device contained a palette of 128 different scented oils. When triggered, iSmell would internally combine selected smells and expel a puff of scent.

So yeah, here's something that's both really cool while simultaneously intensely stupid.

The idea was that there would be *smell-enabled* games—smell the caverns, the sweat, the dead bodies . . . Problem is, even with their seventy employees and $20 million in funding, they never got around to releasing the thing.

Besides, potential customers weren't too keen on having a bunch of nasty-smelling chemicals pumped up their noses.

Another idea was that perfume websites would smell like perfume. Okay . . . just a thought here, but would a company like, say, Gucci, trust this little box to accurately reproduce their fragrance? And if so, wouldn't people then just use the fuckin' smell from the box rather than actually buying the perfume? Further still, WHO THE FUCK GOES TO PERFUME WEBSITES. We can't leave out the obvious . . .

Still, this is cool, but so far the only applications that anyone can think of don't translate to $$$.

That's until now. I propose BURNINGSHITBAG.COM. This is a virtual burning bag of shit, delivered right to the email box of your favorite fucked CEO. The synergies are "overpowering" and the market seems just right.

URINALCAKES.COM coming soon.

FLOOZ.COM

Since the day they received funding, Flooz was my example of how people would invest in the stupidest of ideas, so long as it involved the Internet.

Flooz was an *alternative currency.* The idea is that people would buy FLOOZ, and then use FLOOZ to buy stuff, rather than using CREDIT CARDS or CASH. But the thing was, you could only spend your stupid-ass Flooz at participating online retailers—all sixty-five of 'em or whatever.

Hey stop laughing, it's true. Investors pushed $51.5 million in three rounds down this crap hole.

Funny thing was, it seemed even Flooz itself couldn't figure out a way to justify their existence. I mean really, who on Earth would use it? The best answer the company could come up with was "procrastinating gift-givers." You know, it's 10 P.M. the night before Christmas and you forgot to get Mom a present—I know, email her some Flooz! (That sounds so dirty.)

I always thought it would be a fun, cruel joke to buy a friend some Flooz as a gift. It's like, "It's *almost* money, 'cept you can't hardly use it anywhere, and you gotta act quick cuz this baby is sinking fast!"

I mean, why trust the U.S. Treasury to back your money when there's FLOOZ! The company would go on and on about their retail partners, but their "partners" were nothing more than companies that Flooz could sweet-talk into adding a friggin "Flooz" option under the "Visa" and "MasterCard" options.

Flooz filed for Chapter 7 bankruptcy protection on August 31, 2001. Their main competitor, the equally stupid Beenz.com, closed shop the same month. Glad they folded before the rest of the world converted all their currency to Beenz, Flooz, and Chuck E. Cheese video game tokens . . .

Money Shot

Well it seemed Flooz was useful for at least one thing—credit-card fraud.

Sources close to the company said that thieves in Russia and the Philippines were using stolen credit-card numbers to load up on Flooz, almost $300,000 worth.

See *ExchangePath.com* for more on that . . .

MR. SWAP

Mister Swap . . . so *this* was a dumb idea . . . it was a swapping service, specializing in swapping music, videos, and video games from user to user. Barter . . . Its mission was to enable "cashless" transactions.

But thank goodness communism was avoided. The evil plans of MrSwap.com to create a cashless society of the Beast Satan 666 has been thwarted by the good white Christian men of America, praised be Jesus!

Swappers paid $2.99 for a cardboard mailer with $1.21 postage on it. That was the big revenue model. That brilliance is how MrSwap.com raised almost $5 million funding.

"The reason for this is simple. The company was unable to achieve profitability before our financing ran out," it said on their site. Well at least they didn't blame it on "market conditions" . . . even if they *were* communists.

Here's a little hint for all you potential investors out there: If a business plan includes the word "cashless" anywhere in its text, don't walk—run!

12:00 noon Pacific, July 30, 2001, it ended.

E VILLA

Would you buy a product called "Evil"?

E Villa was Sony's stab at creating an "Internet appliance," Web-only computer (see *ePods*). It looked like a small computer—monitor . . . mouse . . . keyboard—but it had no real operating system (BeOS in the background), just a web browser and email reader. Booting up was almost instantaneous. The monitor was vertical, portrait orientation, so it could fit more of a website on the screen at once.

It sounds like a good idea, but the weird part is that every year a different company releases a new Internet-only computer, just to find out that nobody wants 'em. Previous failures include Netpliance's iOpener, ePods, 3com's Audrey . . . there are more.

Why? (Here's the part where I start making shit up.)

The E Villa cost $499, plus $21.95 per month for an ISP (no, you couldn't just dial it into your own ISP). So . . . the first year costs $762.40. That's about the price of a middle-of-the-road computer these days—a computer that can do a hell of a lot more than Sony's piece of doo. (100 years from now when this book is required reading in universities—and oh goodness it will be—they'll be laughing at these numbers. Ha. Ha.)

Oh wait scratch that—the reason they've all failed is cuz you can buy a WebTV for $50. Damn those Microsoft people, always ruining everyone's fun . . .

PAPERFLY.COM

"PaperFly is an award winning Application Service Provider providing best-in-class technology for managing business information at the department level and across the enterprise. PaperFly's secure and scalable ASP platform allows enterprises to rapidly deploy business information management solutions that are easy to maintain without increasing investment in IT or training."

PaperFly.com had a vision. A vision of getting pig-dirty rich by dazzling investors with a load of neo-Orwellian

MBA doublespeak for what is essentially a glorified FTP server.

And there we have it, $2 million invested in a fileserver with a web front-end. Thanks, you're dismissed, not missed.

MODO

Another winner founded in part by Idealab, Modo was this little gadget that looked like a pager and displayed information about restaurants, bars, and entertainment in New York City, San Francisco, and Los Angeles.

The device was too clunky to be worth carrying around everywhere, and it simply couldn't compete with similar services that worked with PalmPilots and other more useful handheld devices.

The company went out of business blindingly fast, burning an estimated $40 million and shutting down just five short weeks after it launched—reportedly one day before their official launch party.

EMPORI.COM

"EMPORI.COM changes the online shopping experience by humanizing the Internet with real people and real places . . ."

I dunno, one of the best things about e-commerce is that I DON'T HAVE TO DEAL WITH STUPID FUCKING PEOPLE when I wanna buy crap. And I don't have to go anywhere. And I don't have to bathe. or wear pants. ever.

Empori.com tried to change all that. bastards.

The deal was that users could buy stuff from the portal on

Empori.com's website, or at any of the actual Empori.com stores, located in office buildings around Canada. The stores didn't have any actual products, but they had customer service people and little web kiosks.

Empori.com didn't actually sell products—rather, they had relationships with online vendors. Products purchased would be shipped same-day or next-day to one of the Empori.com locations. At the Empori.com location, the product was stored in a secure locker, and the shopper was notified via email of the locker location and combination.

So basically . . . they were a temporary storage facility. Like a P.O. Box, but with really expensive real estate and ultramodern, pricey-looking architecture. The largest one was 4,200 square feet. Empori's justification for this fiasco was that they were saving people time by opening their centers in office buildings and subway platforms, so people could just grab their shit on the way home.

But they were really just opening P.O. Boxes with the illusion of being somehow dot-com related. Cuz ya know . . . being dot-com related is hip and gets ya all the chicks I hear . . . (right).

Empori's parent company, Oxford Properties Group, took a $5 million hit on the books for this failed investment.

ARZOO.COM

In 1997, Sabeer Bhatia sold his little website, Hotmail.com, to Microsoft Corp. for $400 million. Never mind the fact that there are a million Web-based email sites *these* days, Hotmail was the first, and in 1997, that meant MAD CRAZY CREAM YO.

Anyway, Arzoo.com was Bhatia's follow-up attempt. It was billed as an intellectual capital marketplace for technologists and engineers, selling answers and ideas as one would sell physical products. Specifically, Arzoo had a network of around 2,000 freelance and full-time "experts" whose job it was to read questions from Arzoo users and answer the questions in a real-time chat or forum type of interface. If the answers were acceptable, the experts got paid.

Now in theory this sounds kinda cool. I mean, a site where you could go to find out the answer to anything technical.

Wait, there's already a site like that. It's called THE INTERNET. Maybe you've heard of it.

Not only that, but you've also got access to thousands of specialized, free message boards, forums, chat services, and all-encompassing knowledge bases like Everything2.com.

I'm a huge proponent of charging for stuff that's generally given away for free on the Web, but Arzoo might actually be the first dot-bomb example I can think of where they were CHARGING for something that I truly believe SHOULD be free.

And WAS free.

For what little value that they added, Arzoo charged businesses anywhere between $50 and $100,000 to use the service. Thing is, the Internet is already set up for—was DESIGNED for—the free flow of information and ideas. That said, GOOGLE should charge money—*that* we'd all pay for.

On a side note (not really), Arzoo users had to download and install a 200kb plug-in just to use the thing. Now that's just silly.

When Arzoo closed their site, they blamed their failure on the "severe downturn in the U.S. economy." For the life of me I can't figure out what the U.S. economy had to do with their site not catching on, but hey whatever floats your boat.

PNV.COM

From their site, *"PNV is the leading provider of bundled telecommunications, cable television and Internet access services to truck drivers in the privacy and convenience of their truck cabs."*

WHAT THE FUCK, GET YOUR EYES ON THE ROAD AND YOUR HANDS BACK ON THE GODDAM WHEEL YOU METH-ADDLED PORN ADDICTS.

Look, I'm all for Internet access, but NOT WHILE YOU'RE DRIVING 80,000 POUNDS OF RIG OVER MY CAR.

XIGO.COM

Xigo.com was a silly little company (okay $22 million and eighty-five people . . . not so little) that made a free little service where users could sign up for cute little email notifications about their cute little stock portfolios.

Aww, so snuggly.

Notifications could be based on any of a number of triggers such as "Notify me when Company X's price dips below a certain level" or "Notify me when so-and-so rates such-and-such stock a 'strong buy.'"

A perfectly garbage product, financial pornography at its worst.

I mean come on—some slut of a Wall Street "analyst"

raises his rating on a company from "outperform" to "strong buy" and somehow getting this news via email helps you become a better investor?

The people who dreamed up and funded this company are as lame as the people who tried earnestly to use the service.

XFL

XFL, the WWF's "The-X-doesn't-stand-for-anything-it-just-looks-cool Football League," promised mass carnage and hot cheerleader-ass but didn't deliver.

End of story.

CAMPSIX

CampSix was another piece of crap that jumped on the "Internet incubator" bandwagon, only to burn through $20 million, not to mention screwing their portfolio companies.

If you hadn't already caught on that the whole "dot-com" thing was a joke, the proliferation of Internet incubators should clue you in. Basically, they were dot-bomb factories. In exchange for 20% or 30% of the company, an incubator provided office space, a receptionist, office supplies, maybe a common strategic thinker or two, and some funding. Incubators were companies set up to build, launch, and offload these jokes as soon as possible.

Their other purpose? Hype. Incubators had to be masters of hype—that was their only hope of making a buck off fools willing to pay money for the worthless portfolio companies they helped to build.

The company had thirty-five employees and incubated a few tiny shitwad dot-coms all from their posh San Francisco offices . . . In some ways, dot-coms launched with the help of an incubator had even less of a chance. How could an incubator encapsulate and repeat the entrepreneurial spirit that is the key ingredient, the best asset of a startup, good business model or not?

CampSix was named for the last base camp before the summit of Mount Everest.

So basically . . . incubating was a good description—sit on your butt, hope your ass will hatch a million bucks.

COMEDY WORLD

"We're not a dot-com!" they said.

Regardless, Comedy World (a.k.a. ComedyWorld.com) started with a website and pretended to be a dot-com, and thus I gots no problems lumping them in as one. Although they did boast ex-MTV chick Kennedy as a contributor and, call me crazy, she gave me wood . . . but anyway.

But I don't know, you decide: Comedy World produced "funny" content and then sold it to websites and radio stations. Among the HILARIOUS content promised was a virtual cat-fight between the original Charlie's Angels and the cast of the Charlie's Angels movie—the one that featured Cameron Diaz in various revealing outfits. At least, that's what they *claimed*—the outfits weren't all that revealing.

Oh wait we're talking about Comedy World. Right. Oh yeah so anyway my point was that it wasn't funny—something you'd *think* would have been a prerequisite for a company called "Comedy World" . . .

Furthermore, they blamed their demise on the "current climate" and other such fooey . . . could their demise really have anything to do with the fact that not only were they not *funny*, but nobody (a) watches Internet programming or (b) listens to shtick on the radio anymore? Is it fucking 1940? And I'm really giving them too much credit—their original focus was ONLINE radio stations . . . at least they figured that one out . . .

Anyway, $31 million later, the 140 remaining employees (they had almost 180 at one point) were given thirty minutes to pack their shit and leave the building, only to be searched and interrogated by security thugs on the way out.

IEXCHANGE.COM

This is hilarious—and happens to be another masterpiece by incubator Idealab.

Not parody, it's real.

You go to iExchange.com. You pick a few stocks and write little "reports" about each one. Just make up a bunch of bullshit explaining why they're good picks. Use words like "really, really, really" a lot.

Then you get paid.

iExchange actually PAID random people to pick stocks. At one point they were reportedly paying $10 per pick. Elderly housewives in Phoenix were picking stocks based on their pretty logos. Marvelous.

As if that's not enough, iExchange would then attempt to sell this advice to other people, to strangers. Essentially, they compiled the most random, pointless investment advice on the Internet—and attempted to get rich selling it.

The company was financed with $6 million and blew it as fast as humanly possible.

SHOPPINGLIST.COM

Ooh ooh, "clicks-to-bricks"! The idea here is that shoppers would go to ShoppingList.com, type in their ZIP code, and get a list of real, actual stores in their neighborhood that were having sales.

Kinda like a revenue-sharing portal, except there was no way for ShoppingList.com to collect commissions from the stores, because there was no way to prove who bought what as a direct result of the website.

Eventually they tried to get tricky and make deals with brick-and-mortar retailers where ShoppingList.com customers could print coupons off the website, so purchases could be tracked and commissions could be paid.

Never worked though. Stores were used to coupons coming from the manufacturers, who didn't require any commissions be paid—BECAUSE THE STORE BOUGHT THE PRODUCT FROM THEM IN THE FIRST PLACE. There's only so much profit to go around, and apparently not enough for sites like this to dip their hands into.

So they relied on advertising dollars . . . Think about it—if you had a website that listed sales in your area, and stores could pay to be on the list—eventually you'd have a website MADE UP ENTIRELY OF ADVERTISEMENTS. Very useful . . .

The funny part is that no matter what product I typed in, it told me to go to Sears.

I might as well have just gone to Sears.

It makes me think of Times Square in New York City—tons of electronics stores with big "Going out of business! Everything must go!" banners, hoping to attract clueless tourists . . . and impulsive idiots like me, who, despite being ripped off numerous times by these shops, continue to frequent them. But that's another story—most people aren't as dumb as me—so they were doomed from the start.

EPODS

Funded with $2 million from Salton, the company behind the GLORIOUS George Foreman Grill that is the centerpiece of my kitchen, ePods were another one of those "Internet appliances." It was a $199 self-contained device that provided Internet access (web surfing and email) by hooking up to a proprietary Internet service provider via its built-in 56k modem.

The seemingly brilliant idea that set this device apart from its many competitors is that it was to be distributed through infomercials and department stores, rather than through computer stores that tend to intimidate ePods' target market—stupid people.

This piece of crap used an old RISC processor and had a whopping 16 megs of memory, making it pretty useless from the get-go. Plus, with its slow connection, porn surfing would have proved difficult.

And we all know that porn equals success.

CLICKABID.COM

Far as I know, this Canadian auction site was the first site to host its own bankruptcy auction.

HOW ABOOT THAT?

QUESTIONEXCHANGE.COM

What did they do?

QuestionExchange.com was a support forum for open-source-related questions and answers. It was started by Andover.net and then was bought by VA Linux (along with Slashdot, Freshmeat, and some other websites) for roughly $1 billion.

Problem was that anyone with two brain cells or more was able to find everything they needed from either Usenet or a search engine like Google.com.

Question: How did they plan on making money?

I don't know . . . let's ASK THEM! Oh wait, we can't anymore . . . Har har har.

I'm an idiot.

SOURCES

Archive.org
Associated Press
bCentral.com
Business Week
CNET (News.com)
CNN.com
EcommerceTimes.com
ePrairie.com
Fool.com
Google.com
Hoovers.com
The Industry Standard (R.I.P.)
Internet.com
LocalBusiness.com (R.I.P.)
New York Post and Joseph Gallivan

NewsFactor.com
Red Herring
Reuters
Rising Tide Studios (*Silicon Alley Daily, Digital Coast Weekly*)
Salon.com
Slashdot.org
Star-Telegram.com
TechTV
TheCan.org
Upside.com
USA Today
ZDNet.com

That's it . . . now I can finally get back to learning yoga so I can auto-fellate myself.

ACKNOWLEDGMENTS

There are way too many people deserving of my thanks to list here, but here are a few: Gidon Wise, Menachem Dickman, Aryeh Goldsmith, Mike Wise, Kent Klineman, Sam and Leslie Kaplan, Donna LeBlanc, Geoff Kloske and Simon & Schuster, David Vigliano, Dean Williams, Sarah Dolgen and family, Joseph Shireman, Zachariah Nagy, David Lawrence and Lili, Seth and Barbara Kaplan, Marlen Mertz, Laura Axel, Florence and "Willy" Kaplan, Joan Kaplan, Marvin Mostow, Sheila and Steven Meisel, Gay Jervey, Jason Calacanis, Marco Pallotti, Mia Starr, Al Goldstein, Nick Baily, Aron Malkine, Craig Thomas, Marcus Gregory, George Ardeleanou, Bernardo Joselevich, Christine Pascarella and everyone at HostCentric, Maheesh Jain and CafePress.com, Justin Stark, Audre Lukosevicius, Richard Morris, Barry Werbin, Norman Brodsky, Arthur Silbert, Booz Crew, FTG, Stile, MamaSatan, WhineKiller, Cali, Dr. Heathen Scum, and everyone else who's helped along the way.

Extra-special thanks to FC users and the regular FC message board fucknozzles: Thanks for shedding light on these companies and for sharing your opinions—and also for helping with some of the chapter titles, quotes on the back, and for keeping the site interesting . . . and stupid. ;)

COMPANY INDEX

ABOUT THE AUTHOR

In May 2000, having nothing better to do with his Memorial Day weekend, Philip J. Kaplan created Fuckedcompany .com to track the layoffs, the bankruptcies, and the generally bad behavior of dot-com companies. The site became an immediate success and has grown into one of the most well-read news sources on the Web, attracting more than 4 million visitors a month. Fuckedcompany.com was named "Site of the Year" by *Rolling Stone, Time,* and Yahoo!, among others.

Kaplan is also the president of PK Interactive, an e-commerce solutions firm. He lives in New York City and can be seen playing drums in smoky heavy metal clubs around town.